FINISHING TOUCH

A SURVIVOR'S JOURNEY

REGINA LATRICE

forWord BOOKS

John 1:1 In the beginning was the Word...

for**Word**
BOOKS

John 1:1 In the beginning was the Word...

Finishing Touch
A Survivor's Journey
Published by ForWord Books
21143 Hawthorne Blvd, Ste 184
Torrance, CA 90503

Scripture quotations are taken or paraphrased from the following: King James Version, The Holy Bible.

Statistics provided were compiled from the following sources:

Bourgeois, Christen. *Stop Dating Violence Before It Starts*, 9 Feb. 2024, www.hiprc.org/blog/tdvam-2024/. Accessed 1 May 2024.

National Coalition Against Domestic Violence. *NCADV National Statistics Domestic Violence Fact Sheet*, www.ncadv.org/STATISTICS. Accessed 1 May 2024.

Back cover photo by Stan Brock

ISBN 979-8-9882642-7-9

Published in the United States by ForWord Books

DEDICATION

This book is dedicated to every woman and man who has been a victim of domestic violence and divorce. For those who have walked or are currently walking down a path that seems hopeless, I am here to tell you that you are more than a conqueror. You are not a failure. You are not what you've done. We all have made mistakes in life, but the beauty of it all is that God still wants to make a masterpiece out of our pain. You do not have to stay in a toxic unhealthy relationship, no matter what you're reasoning behind it may be: finances, children, loyalty, FEAR. I am here to tell you that it is not God's plan for your life. He will make a way of escape and give you a life that you never imagined. You are worthy of better. You deserve to experience life in a way you never thought was possible. Your freedom is not just about you. There are other people in the world that need hope. I am only one person and can't get this story to everyone. Come on sis, come on bro. Let's join hands and go make a difference in the world. It is God's will for our lives. But if we are too afraid to do what He has called us to do, then we are saying that we do not trust Him at his word. Forgive the person/people who wronged you. I mean, I really forgive them. Forgive yourself. Start to hope and believe again. Follow God's plan for your life and allow Him to put the *Finishing Touch* on your story. Life is out there. It's time to live.

I love you all and thank you for taking the time to consider reading my story. I pray that God was glorified and that you were blessed. There is hope.

Regina Latrice

ACKNOWLEDGMENTS

I am so grateful, honored, and blessed to have been given such an opportunity to share my story of grace, forgiveness, and hope. I am honored to have been trusted with so much pain and the ability to continue to fight through. I never understood why I had to climb so many mountains and fall into so many valleys. I am just blessed to be alive to share my story in a unique and meaningful way.

I would like to first thank the MAN who made it all possible, my Lord and Savior Jesus Christ. Without Him, there is no me or *Finishing Touch*. I am forever grateful for the grace and mercy He has bestowed upon my life. I am not worthy.

I want to thank my mom, Julia, for giving me the gifts that keep on giving; life and Jesus. You have impacted my life in ways that you don't know just because you didn't back down from raising me to love the Lord.

Thank you to my father, Elgin, for everything you have given me. In your weakest and lowest moments, you still found ways to be a blessing to me and my children.

To my lovely children, thank you for sticking with me. Thank you for the right words, hugs, kisses, and words of encouragement at the right time. You guys are my reason for being and fighting and I thank you all for loving me at my lowest moments.

To my sisters and brothers, Bettye Nicole, Roberta, Tiara, Unecia, Angela, Stephen, Stan, and Willie, thank you guys for always being willing to help me in times of need and never complaining but always stepping up.

To my besties, Tweet and Jameshia, you guys already know the roles you played in my walk to freedom. You're the true definition of true loyal friends. I love you guys beyond words.

To my friend Dennis Love, thank you for the role you have played in my life and my children's lives.

Last, but certainly not least, thank you to Larry, Paris, and Langston at ForWord Books publishing company. I am grateful for you guys trusting me and opening up the door for me to share my testimony. There are no words to express how thankful I am.

Thanks to all of my supporters for pushing me to believe in myself when I couldn't see past the failures. To my pastors, counselors, associates, and mentors, thank you all for the love. All of you guys saw something in me that I couldn't see. I am just filled with gratitude.

TABLE OF CONTENTS

INTRODUCTION
viii

CHAPTER ONE
THE JOURNEY BEGINS
2

CHAPTER TWO
A MOTHER'S GOTTA DO WHAT A MOTHER'S GOTTA DO
12

CHAPTER THREE
GUILT AND GRACE
23

CHAPTER FOUR
GOD'S TRYING TO TELL ME SOMETHING
34

CHAPTER FIVE
BOY LET'S JUST GET MARRIED
45

CHAPTER SIX
A CAR CAN'T BUY YOU LOVE
55

CHAPTER SEVEN
A LEOPARD DOESN'T LOSE ITS SPOTS
62

CHAPTER EIGHT
YOU GOT SERVED
72

CHAPTER NINE
MY EXODUS
80

CHAPTER TEN
TRUTH SPEAKS FOR ITSELF
86

CHAPTER ELEVEN
THE PERFECT MISFIT
91

CHAPTER TWELVE
FEAR IS NOT MY FUTURE
95

CHAPTER THIRTEEN
OLD WAYS WON'T OPEN NEW DOORS
101

CHAPTER FOURTEEN
STRENGTH LIKE NO OTHER
106

CHAPTER FIFTEEN
THE FINISHING TOUCH
112

INTRODUCTION

Welcome to *Finishing Touch: A Survivor's Journey*. This book is written with the intent to bring hope after domestic violence. Hope after divorce. Hope after failure. Hope after what seemed like death. The words "finishing touch" can be defined as a final detail or action completing and enhancing a piece of work. I have walked the path of being a victim of domestic violence in my marriage. I felt so lost, ugly, and unworthy. Once my divorce was finalized, I didn't know what my next season of life would look like.

I am so excited about this book and how God showed me myself through a new lens. He allowed me to go through a season of learning who I am and who I was really created to be. He took the broken pieces of my life and put the finishing touch on them. I now see myself in the beauty of His holiness and it has been an amazing experience. I have walked a tedious long hard journey.

In this book, I will share my story in a graceful God-glorifying way. I hope you enjoy it.

"...THE RACE IS NOT TO THE SWIFT, NOR THE BATTLE TO THE STRONG,..."

ECCLESIASTES 9:11

1

THE JOURNEY BEGINS

My name is Regina Latrice Johnson. I am a single mom of three beautiful, amazing children. Leslie Jr is 18 years old and the sweetest most caring young man I have ever met. Jakirah is 17 years old and is my mini-me. Like for real, she is so smart, responsible, and helpful. Jaleah is 12 years old and has the most beautiful spirit, eyes, and sense of humor. I had my son when I was 16 years old. Yes, I was a teen mom. I grew up in a house full of loving but annoying siblings. We were not as close as we are now but you could always feel the love there. My mom has seven biological children and three that are adopted. They are all biological siblings. My father was also in the household. Not consistently, but he was there. My father suffered from alcoholism. My mom is a phenomenal woman. The strength that she has is like no other. She did the best she could to raise my siblings and me. We didn't have the best childhood or the finest things, but I am grateful. As children, none of us really had healthy relationships with our fathers. But I must say, we all turned out alright.

As a little girl, I was always longing to be "Daddy's little girl." Between the movies I watched, and being around other little girls who had those relationships, it was a desire of mine. Yes, I loved my mommy but the daddy-daughter relationship for some reason seemed to hit differently. Because of my relationship with my father, I became curious about a lot of things in life. I felt different and like something was wrong with me because of the rejection. I have always had the feeling of being different and like

I just didn't belong. I think that this is the starting point in my life where the spirit of loneliness and feeling unloved began. Pretty much in my mind, I was a failure. Oh, by the way, I was the little bright-skinned girl with really fat cheeks; that caused insecurities and I would get teased at school.

I became curious about what my adult life would look like. When I was around other adults, I used to say I can't wait to be grown. I wanted to have that feeling of independence and create a life opposite of what I've always known. I wanted to have a family of my own and be able to live comfortably financially. As I stated earlier, my mom did the best she could. It was hard going to school with used Goodwill clothes (now I love thrifting clothes) and Walmart tennis shoes. Seeing other children in the finer things put a desire in my heart to want to be able to see what it's like. I remember lying at school about my mom stating she would buy me some Jordans or take me on a shopping spree. I just wanted to be relevant. Now looking back, it was foolish of me to do that. But that kind of pressure as a kid was no joke.

My mom is the sweetest, most selfless woman anyone would ever meet. Through all of my struggles and hers, she continues to show great strength. When I was around 13 years old, my sister, who I believe was 17 at the time, was shot in a drive-by shooting. She was paralyzed from the waist down. I remember that night like yesterday. My mom got the call from my oldest sister, who was also with her at the time she was shot. I remember my mom instantly getting on her knees, crying out to God before we left to go to the hospital. The entire ride there was nerve-wracking. I was in shock and didn't even cry or anything because I just didn't know what to feel. We got to one hospital and they told us she was being airlifted to another one in Missouri for surgery. The bullet had traveled into her spine, which is what caused the paralysis. I remember being in the waiting room, just sitting and watching everyone react. Again, I didn't even know how to begin to react. When the doctor finally came out to report the surgery was a success, he stated that she'd never be able to walk again. Like what??? How did this just suddenly happen? I felt so bad and sad for my mother. I knew this was about to change all of our lives. But I am grateful that my sister made it through.

This is a time I remember myself showing great strength and also leadership. See, I stepped in to really help my mom with the household. I started doing more cleaning and cooking for the house. I just felt like I needed to make the load lighter for my mom. She was, of course, basically living at the facilities with my sister until she was able to come home. It was a long, scary road. Complications arose but God kept my sister in His hands. When my sister was able to come home, I helped my mom with her care as much as I could. I never complained because I felt like that was the least I could do. I couldn't imagine being in that state at such a young age. This caused me to also want to be a doctor or nurse. I felt like it was my calling. I actually enjoyed helping and taking care of someone who wasn't fully able to do for themself.

All things were good but it also caused even more emotions in me. You see, I was very understanding of the situation but I also felt like I didn't matter. My sister received so much attention, and rightfully so. But I felt the rejection and a sense of unworthiness. I mean my mom had to literally give her 24-hour care so that took attention away from the other kids. Again, I say rightfully so. So, no one intentionally did anything to harm me. The circumstances were unfortunate but it did affect me. I love my sister so much and we have grown very close over the last few years. God is amazing. She is still here and a true champion. Because my mom's attention was limited towards me, this caused me to be able to kind of do some sneaky things. I didn't think back then that this was wrong, but oh how I regret it so badly. I used a tragic situation to do what I wanted. I'm still paying for that decision.

Now let's get into the start of this relationship that would cause my life to have some hard consequences. I was in middle school when I met some amazing young ladies. We are still friends to this day. We have always been jokesters and play a whole lot. We became really close. We would often hang out in these projects right outside of middle school. Yes, we were young and fast (*laugh out loud*). So, boys were a thing for us. Well...them. I was innocent and quiet (*laugh out loud*). There was a group of guys that hung out together just like we did. We would play and tell these guys that one of us liked him just to see what would happen. There was this one guy out of the bunch that none of my friends thought was attractive. See me, I have never been the woman who cared too much about looks. I was teased as a child so I just wanted everyone to be kind and I was not the one to call anyone unattractive. They would always crack jokes and say they were going to tell him I liked him. He wore this blue coat that stood out. It was more on the purple side in my friend's eyes. They were not fans. Well, one day we were all on one side of the building and they yelled to him, "Regina said she likes you and your purple coat." I looked at them like why would y'all do that. But whatever, it's just fun.

Often on the weekend, we would all go to the skating rink and the entire school basically would be there. I remember him being there one night and he walked up to me and said, "I heard you liked me." I believe I gave him my number or vice versa. That's where the fire started. This is when I began to lie to my mom about being with my friends after school and begging her to let me stay in the projects for a while. It was easy for me to do this because like I said, she was there with my sister a whole lot. I became closer and closer with this guy to the point I really believed I was in love. How foolish. He came from a broken home so we started to depend

5

on one another for comfort.

I lost my virginity at the age of 13. I knew nothing about sex. No one had ever talked to me about it. But when I think about it, it wasn't time. I was literally still a kid. One of my big cousins lived out in the projects and she would allow me to stay at her house with him in exchange for babysitting her children. So that was another easy way for me to convince my mom to let me be out there. My cousin did eventually stop allowing it because it became a party house and she wasn't having that.

We found ways to always make it work. He had a friend who also lived there. His mom worked evenings, so literally everyone would be there with their partners almost every day with no supervision, or, of course, we would go to his home which was not far from the school. Eventually, the word got out to the family that I was seeing this guy. Of course, I was in denial but they knew. My oldest sister and her kids' father would often come up to me out there. I felt ashamed. I knew what I was doing was wrong. I was obsessed with this guy, lying to my mom, and having sex; not even knowing what I was really doing. Things between us became serious. I started to see some things that I blew off. He was manipulative and deceitful. He also had serious anger issues. He would get mad at simple things. Like me spilling food on the bed or me making certain statements. I felt like more of his mother than girlfriend. I would make sure we had food after school and money for whatever we needed. I felt like the caretaker. This is what I was doing at home so it spilled over. I would buy him clothes, pay his phone bill, and all kinds of things. I don't even remember how I even had the funds to do this stuff but I did. His mom worked a lot and he would tell me he doesn't have anyone and how much he needs me.

The honeymoon phase of the relationship didn't last long. He became abusive. I know this sounds crazy because I was a kid.

As I stated earlier, he came from a broken home. He had many traumatic experiences as a child. He also battled with some of the same mental battles I did. He felt rejected, unloved, unwanted, and he also was teased about the way he looked and his clothing. Connecting with him gave us both a sense of belonging. By the time I realized he had some real anger issues, I felt trapped and like I couldn't let go. He became not only verbally abusive but also physically abusive. I remember being in class with bruises on my arm and this girl sitting next to me whispering to her friend, "She has bruises on her arm." That was so embarrassing. I'm in the eighth grade dealing with abuse in a way like never before. I knew I needed to get away, but did the opposite. I tried everything I could to stay around and close. My mom at this time had moved my family from East St. Louis, Illinois to St. Louis, Missouri. I completed my eighth-grade school year in Missouri. But I knew that wasn't going to work if I was going to be close to him. I quickly figured out a way to be able to attend high school with him. He was attending the alternative school, not the regular high school, and I made my way there. He was a year ahead of me, so when I got there to the school, I quickly learned about many other young women he was dealing with. It was not what I thought. I felt used because although for that one year I transferred, I still made my way to see him and help him however I could. It was a huge mistake for me to go to that school. It just gave me more of a reason to be upset and for him to abuse me.

I remember one of the first times he hit me. I pulled up to the residence he was staying at. He wasn't answering my calls. I knocked on the door and the man living there came to answer. The door had bars on it so he had to go get the key to unlock it. So once I got into the house, I found him in there with another girl. One I knew from school, and she would always speak to me as if we were besties. Of course, I became upset and left. I headed to the Metrolink to get on the train to go back home. He got into the car he was driving, chased me, pulled me into the car, and took me back to his house. He accused me of intentionally making him upset and started punching me in my arms and legs. He would always hit me in places where I could hide the marks. We would then have sex afterward, and he would apologize. He would also use the 'you're going to leave me knowing I don't have anyone else' speech. That actually worked. I thought, I know how it feels to be in that position; to feel like nobody sees you; to feel like the little love from anyone is better than feeling alone. The toxic cycle had just begun. Now, here I am just a child, but really in an adult relationship. I'm being abused, cheated on, lied about, and used. What do I do though?

He had one really close friend. He was actually living with him at this time. He knew about the abuse and would make it known to others. So, people knew, but, of course, I was always in denial. It's always good to have genuine people around you. My friends would talk to me and tell me that wasn't ok and that I shouldn't be sticking around. While I thought I was doing good by keeping things a secret, I was harming myself even more by continuing to live in denial. Fast forward a few years ahead, I turned 15 years old and, not surprisingly, found out I was pregnant. I was so embarrassed. I felt like a failure, ashamed, and hopeless. I tried my best to keep it a secret. I knew my family would be disappointed. They knew of the abuse and lies at this point, and they didn't approve of him. Rightfully so. Word started spreading fast, and so did I. I kept being in denial. I remember my mom calling me saying, jokingly, "What's this I hear about you being pregnant?" My heart dropped, and, of course, I denied it. More than anything I didn't want to put my mom through anything more than what she was already dealing with. But what can I do at this point? She was already struggling to take care of the family. I was just a broke kid

8

with no job, and no idea about life or being a parent. How did I get into this situation with this young man? I told him about the pregnancy and he instantly denied it was his and didn't want anything to do with me. I remember feeling so disgusting and ashamed. After my mom called, and he denied that it was his, I tried to figure out a way to get rid of the pregnancy. At this point, I was a good four months into it. I researched on Google how to have a miscarriage. I drank vinegar and even punched myself in the stomach a few times. Nothing happened. I just couldn't fathom how miserable my life was about to be. Now looking back, that was one of the most foolish things I've ever done. I could have damaged my son. God is amazing. He covered me.

Eventually, the truth came out and everyone knew I was having a baby. He was still dodging me so one day my friends and I went to his sister's home. She was outside and I got out to speak and told her I was pregnant. She was shocked. She called her mom and told her I believe. But eventually, he called me because the family knew. He started to come back around just a bit. He went to the last few doctor appointments, but he didn't show much interest in being a father. But the thought in my mind was, whatever, as long as he's here. This didn't stop anything he had going on. The fights continued. We fought so badly one day because he was talking to another girl on the phone while I was next to him. I got up to leave while I was about six months pregnant. He was angry. He started punching me in the stomach while calling me every name but Regina. I wanted this to be over. I would often ask myself why my life is like this. What did I do to deserve this? God would deal with me even in those moments. Although my childhood wasn't the greatest, I knew better. All of the church and good teaching my mom put in me were in my consciousness. I couldn't blame my parents or anyone else. God kept giving me ways of escape but I would find my way back to it. Every time there was separation, although I knew it was good, I felt uncomfortable. I didn't want to be alone so I would rather get beat. Separation hurts, loneliness hurts. Who wants to be alone now, especially being a pregnant teen? But I can honestly say I have always had the best support system: no judgment, but wisdom from both my family and friends. My aunt even gave me a baby shower at her home with my friends. The love was always genuine.

I

AM

VERY

RESILIENT.

2

A MOTHER'S GOTTA DO
WHAT A MOTHER'S GOTTA DO

I had my son on September 6, 2005. It was a beautiful moment. I had no idea what I was doing, but I was grateful for a healthy baby boy. I knew I would figure the mom thing out. My main goal was just to first love him. My mom was the epitome of what it looked like to love someone unconditionally. His dad wasn't at the birth because he was afraid when I went into labor at my cousin's house and ran out the door. She picked him up after the delivery and he seemed to be madly in love with his baby boy. I thought to myself, God, maybe this is what is needed for him to realize he needs to change his ways. Yes, we are both teens, but now we have another human depending on us. Maybe he will desire to raise his child better than he was. Maybe he won't take the same approach he's witnessed in his upbringing. Nope, once again that was all just a figment of my imagination.

So now, here I am, a single teen mom. I had no idea what I was doing, but I was determined to figure it out. He wasn't around much at all, nor did he give a lot of financial assistance. I got my first job working at McDonald's. I also applied for all of the government assistance that I qualified for to take care of my son. It was nowhere close to what I thought things would be like. Luckily, I had siblings and my mom who was helping me, free of charge, when I needed to work. I was very vulnerable and naive. I continued to chase him despite him choosing not to be there. I would do whatever to have him talk to me, be with me, and want me. I was numb to abuse and any idea that I was worthy of proper treatment. Not to mention now having a child made it even harder

12

to leave. I was willing to do whatever to make this family work. Yes, that included forgetting myself and what made me happy.

People who didn't know our situation always came up to me complimenting us. I would always paint a picture on social media as if we were this happy family. I would even make posts on his page as if he were writing sweet messages to me. I made sure we took plenty of pictures doing fun family things. Behind the scenes, the entire time, it was the total opposite. Even when we went out in public, an argument always occurred. I was constantly finding ways to secure his presence. He would also like the things I did as far as outings and making sure we had different experiences. There were simple things that were shocking for him, like just going to a nice restaurant. Neither of us had much of that growing up. He would also always lie and paint images about his life and the things he had to impress others. He majorly exaggerated. So, I knew that if I planned things, he was going to for sure show up to brag about it later. He also would stay around me when he knew I would be the one spending money for him to enjoy, whether that was a trip to the mall or to eat.

When I started working, I also received cash benefits from the government for my son. I would get that check and my work checks and spend them on him and our son. There would be things that I would desire for myself but I put it on the back burner for them. Imagine being the one paying for clothes, underwear, and food for a guy, and all the while he's using you for that moment. He gives you a little of his time, you don't hear from him for weeks, but you find out he's with other females. Yes, this is when I learned that money can't buy you love.

At some moments, I felt like I had to accept the hand that I pretty much dealt myself. God didn't give me life with him. God wouldn't bring me anything or anyone that would harm me. God's plan and will for me are perfect. So, I understood that there would be consequences for my decisions. I also had this feeling in the back of my mind that I would be accountable for the way that I treated him. See, growing up, my dad was not the nicest person to my mother. Oftentimes, she was being disrespected and abused verbally. She knew that her children witnessing this made us feel horrible. Sometimes we may even say something to my dad about it, which made it even worse for the entire house. She would often respond to him and say, "God doesn't like that, and you will pay for it." She would also say, "I'm going to continue to do good and right by you because I'm responsible for me." That's one of the many things my mother said that stuck with me, even though it was a result of a bad situation. Even though I know what my mother told me was true, I still shouldn't have used that as justification to be abused. I know that the Bible says in 1 Corinthians 7:14, *"For the unbelieving husband is sanctified by the wife..."* I think I took that scripture too seriously because although it says that, there is also much more in the Word that teaches us the correct way to be handled, and that way is God's way. I applied that scripture to my life because as I aforementioned, I witnessed my mother do it, and it seemed to be the right thing to do, but I also wanted to continue to feel comfortable staying in the toxic relationship.

Learning and adjusting to this new life was definitely a journey, but I felt like I was making it. Well, not long after, here we were again. I found out a little while after my son turned one year old that I was pregnant again. Needless to say, I was still having unprotected sex and still uneducated about the options available to prevent getting pregnant. No one really talked to me about sex, and I really didn't blame them before I got pregnant because I was so young and innocent. I get it. I didn't expect that, but then again, I should've because I was repeating the same cycle. So yes, I could believe it. How embarrassing yet again. I was 16 years old with one child, who was broke and lost, and I had the nerve to get pregnant again. I battled mentally with this for so long. There was always someone talking about me having a child at such a young age. I know my family, especially my mom, had to deal with others having something to say about my situation. But it was my fault. I knew better. The guilt of it all wouldn't let me live peacefully. God had given me grace to make it through a healthy pregnancy with my son. He had brought me people in my life who genuinely embraced me and my son. But I am letting everyone down, including myself, is what I thought. I couldn't shake the feeling. I knew sex before marriage was not honorable to God, yet I continued doing so. I've learned that every time we decide to go against the will of God for our lives, we will suffer major consequences, every single time. No one is going to be perfect, but as much as we can, it's important to follow the order in which God instructed.

My family was there for me with my son; sacrificing so much to help me and doing whatever was needed. But why would I continue to take my help for granted? I decided that I was not going to tell anyone that I was pregnant. That's all that I decided in the beginning. I had no idea how I was going to hide my pregnancy, but I was determined to figure it out. I started to gain weight and, of course, it became obvious that I was pregnant. I even found myself doing the same foolish things I had done to try to cause a miscarriage with my son. Of course, it didn't work. But why would it? It didn't work the previous time. I stayed in denial every time someone would ask me. I started to wear bigger clothes and waist trainers to keep my stomach flat. Somehow in my mind, I believed I would be able to keep this a secret for nine months. If you're wondering, no, I didn't even tell him. I'm quite sure everyone close to me knew, but I was able to conceal my pregnancy until it was time to deliver. I never went to any doctor's appointments or anything after I initially found out I was pregnant. I definitely made some unwise decisions that could've been detrimental to myself and my child.

One night I woke up in the middle of the night silently screaming in so much pain. I woke my mom up and told her I needed to go to the hospital because I believed I had another bladder infection. If you have never had one of those, you wouldn't understand. Those were painful enough to make a grown man cry. My mom called me a cab and told me to call her when I got there. I convinced her to let me go alone. So, I got there and could barely get out of the car. The pain was worsening. It felt like the baby was going to come out at any moment. I was thinking to myself the whole time that I was a true soldier. I'm in labor with no medications to ease the pain. I finally got into the room and they rushed me to labor and delivery. I wasn't at the hospital more than ten minutes before I gave birth. Here I am at the hospital with a new beautiful baby girl. I turned my head when they tried to show me her because, in my mind, I already had a plan. There is no way I can go home with a child after lying to everyone. How would I even begin to explain that? The crazy thing is she was born on the exact same day as my son; September 6, 2006. They were exactly one year apart. God is funny, right?

I felt alone in the process, but I handled it the best way I could. Here I am failing again, but I'm about to make this all go away. I thought to myself the only option was to give her up to someone who could really care for her. She deserves the best. I am already struggling trying to figure my life out; barely able to provide for one kid. I had the nurses keep her in the nursery as long as they could. I lay in bed thinking that time was passing and I needed to get back home. Back then you stayed in the hospital at least three days before being released. I knew I had to hurry and get home. My family would become suspicious, and it was my son's first birthday. I had a party planned for a few days after. Surely, I

16

wouldn't be in the hospital for days for a bladder infection. I had called my mom to let her know that I was getting fluids and meds through an IV because the infection was that bad so I would be there awhile. When the nurse came back into the room, I whispered to her "What if I wanted to give her up for adoption?" Tears rolled down my face as I asked. Like, I'm really considering this. I remember she looked over at me with a blank stare and said, "You mean like really give her up for adoption?" I said, "Yes." I told her I didn't want anyone to know. She asked me if I had any family that I wanted to speak with first. I said, "No, I don't want anyone to know." She stated that she would have the social worker come in and talk to me. I asked her how long it would take because I needed to get home to my son and family. I felt defeated and like I needed something to help me numb the pain and guilt. I just knew that my daughter was a princess and deserving of much more than I could ever begin to give her. When I think back I was making a very unwise emotional decision out of fear.

The social worker finally came in and I was able to share my thoughts with her. I wasn't the parent who was just going to allow them to make all of the decisions. Although at the time I was young and foolish, I still cared and wanted the best for my child. I told her I wanted to be fully involved in the adoption process and I wanted to pick the family. I didn't care too much about the race or anything. I just wanted her to be well-loved and wanted the family to be financially ok. The social worker set everything up pretty quickly. I did my part with all of the paperwork. I was able to leave although they suggested that I stay overnight, but I wasn't going to do that. I had a sick, nauseous feeling as I left. Like, I can't believe that I am actually stooping this low. I am a liar and the worst parent a child could

17

ever think about having. That's all that I thought about.

I finally made it back home after having the social worker get me a cab because I lied and said my family didn't have a car. I remember walking into the house and my sister saying, "Your stomach is smaller, you had the baby." First of all, why would that be the first thing you say when you see me in front of everyone? But no, seriously, I felt fire rush through my body. All I could think about is that I was really that dumb to believe no one recognized that I was pregnant. My other siblings started making the same statements, but I was able to change the subject and shake it off. I threw every piece of paperwork in the trash and I made sure that it was shredded. So, I'm thinking ok, I made it through again. Nobody knows but God, me, and the hospital staff. I was walking around like a zombie. I remember days when I would just stay in the bathroom and cry. All I could think about was my beautiful little girl. Every time I looked at my son, I was reminded of her. They looked just alike. It was scary.

There were court meetings and some at the adoption office that I had to attend during the process. It was crazy how I was able to make them all without anyone knowing. I realize now I have always been a little smart and I can think critically and fast when needed. I didn't expect the process to be so tedious. I thought it would be more like a wham bam, thank you ma'am process. But eventually, they found the perfect family for my daughter. After about six months, we were finally getting ready to seal the deal. It was an older Caucasian woman who really wanted her. I met her at one of the final meetings at the office and I felt her genuine heart. She was already caring for my daughter as a foster parent but decided she wanted to have her permanently. I would always receive pictures from her and I would cry and smile at the same time. My daughter seemed so happy. Honestly, she seemed more at peace than me. I know she was a baby, but I always felt like she was in great hands. I was so happy that God placed it on my heart to do an open adoption, although I knew nothing about any of it or how the process worked. I just knew that I needed to make that clear to them in the beginning.

I would be lying if I said I wasn't hurt, but at this point, I had mastered hiding pain. I always thought about how I needed to make better life decisions because my children were really suffering. Again, I knew my daughter was in great hands, but when she gets older, there will be lots of questions. She is going to quickly figure out that the family she was with was not hers originally. She was a very bright-skinned child like myself, but come on, we all know that wouldn't fly. I thought about how that would make her feel. I know the feeling of rejection; feeling unloved; and unwanted, and now, I'm passing these unhealthy feelings down to an innocent child. I thought about how she would feel knowing she had a brother that I kept and a different family.

My spirit was broken and I started to regret the decision I made even more. I had no one going through this process with me, so I was making decisions based on what I was told. We reached the point where I believe I had signed off to where I couldn't make changes. I came to grips with it and figured I would deal with it later. But God! I got a call from my children's father one day out of the blue. I hadn't heard from him in a while. He was yelling, saying, "I got this paper in the mail that says I have a daughter." My heart skipped about five beats, I'm pretty sure. He said he had to go to court (the actual court date to finalize the adoption) if he wanted to appeal. I didn't even realize when I filled out the paperwork at the hospital that I put his info on the forms as the father. That is how they were able to locate him. Now, at this point, he was stating that he wasn't going to let anyone have his daughter and was talking negatively about me. I felt ashamed, but I knew I was making the decision based on what I felt was best for her.

Let me say this, I commend him for even having the mindset to want to fight for her. I can say that, honestly, that was a blessing for me, because I really desired to be with my child. We had our last court hearing. Now, I still hadn't told anyone in my family about what was going on. I get to court and he is there with his older sister and I believe another family member. They were not so happy to see me and I totally understand why. But today his family and I are good. I love them and they love me back. But anywho. We went to court and he ended up winning and taking my daughter with him. In court, they tried their best to deem him as unfit. Although he wasn't the best parent to my son and really showed no support, I wasn't going to speak against him in this situation. Many other young men would not have even put up the effort, so I was grateful for that.

He took my daughter home with him, and she lived there for a while. I made sure she had the things she needed. I remember the first time I brought her to my mom's house. I told my family that it was his baby and that her mom had passed, and I was helping him take care of her. If you could see this child, she looks just like me and my son. It was unbelievable. I know my family thought I was crazy because they obviously knew. I was able to continue with that lie for a moment, but then they put two and two together, and my mom asked me if it was my baby. She mentioned how I was big, went to the hospital, and came home smaller. She was saying that my hospital story wasn't adding up. So, I finally told the truth, and when my daughter was about ten months old, she came home with me. A big weight was lifted. It was time for me to finally face the truth. I made everyone believe a lie, even my friends. They actually teased me for years about lying, saying the mother was deceased. I am a huge jokester, but I didn't find that funny. At the time, I was battling mentally and attempting to move forward with my life, and all that did was bring back memories and thoughts.

20

Now granted, they didn't know any better. Not too long ago they made a joke about it again. I will eventually have a conversation with them about how it makes me feel, or maybe they are reading this book right now and will get the picture (*laugh out loud*). I love y'all and you know exactly who you are.

SOME OF THE THINGS THAT HAPPENED TO ME WERE NOT MY FAULT.

3

GUILT AND GRACE

I never thought the day would come that I would be writing this. No one really knows all of these details outside of my ex and his family. I never talked about it in full detail. He used it for his ego though. When I would argue with him about the lack of care and support he was giving to the children, he brought up the fact that I didn't want my daughter, and how he had to spend so much on fighting for her; which was absolutely false. He even told my daughter one time that I didn't want her and I gave her away to some White people. Just imagine your child hearing that and already dealing with other emotional battles. I told her not to listen to him. But I will present the information to her the right way. Before this book is released, she will know the full truth, and I pray that she understands that at the time, I did what I believed was best for her. She is a true blessing in my life and I am so grateful that the fight for her happened. I am glad to be writing this because there is another level of freedom that comes from me being truthful about my life. God is amazing.

Ok, so let's fast forward now that the cat is out of the bag. I felt like the initial feeling of embarrassment had passed. I continued to be in a relationship with my children's father. I felt like I had no choice but to make it work, especially since there were now two children involved. I started to believe in my mind that I was in a good position. We now have two children. There is no way he will ever leave me. Even if he continues to deal with multiple women, I will always be number one because of the kids. I felt like I had a special place in his heart, so that made me feel superior. People around me at school and in some of my friend groups would even say, "Y'all have children together now, so no matter what he does, he will always put you first. Those other girls have no chance." That made me comfortable for the moment, not to mention the compliments that were posted on social media about how loving and beautiful the family was. I was so bound in my mind with that kind of thinking.

I can say for a while, things seemed to be going smoothly between us, but we all know that a leopard never loses its spots. I confronted him about dealing with other females and that's when the fighting became worse. I am not sure if the pressure of the two small children took a toll on him or what. I know for myself, I was just busy and focused on trying to figure this thing out and not on the circumstances. When I confronted him, he put his hands on me in a different way. I really can't explain it, but it was in a more serious way than before. It was pretty scary. I felt like I was being abused by real demons. By this time in our relationship, he began to drink and smoke. We were young. I believe he was 17 at the time, but those habits had started. So, I was dealing with something different. He would use those things to cope with his struggles and for pleasure as well. I knew from growing up with my dad how bad alcohol was and the effect of it when you are intoxicated. When he would hit me, now his eyes would turn red and it was like he blacked out. I couldn't understand how he could be so selfish and upset with me because I was questioning him about his wrongdoing. I felt fear in the worst way.

During these verbal and physical altercations, he would mention how bad of a person I was because I gave my daughter away. I mean he never stopped. I believe he wanted to make himself look like the father he portrayed to be to others, so that was a great way for him to shame me. His guilt trip started to trigger a lot of emotional and mental torture in me. I felt so ashamed, I can cry right now just thinking about it. I was just a young woman who was trying to find her way and to do the best that I could for my family with the little that I had. Satan had an agenda to attack my life by using him. He knew the plans and purposes that God had for me. I was going through heavy warfare back then. I cried and prayed so much, but the prayers were not the right ones. I asked God continuously to save him so that we could be a good happy family. I wanted God to change him so bad that I was willing to do whatever. I just wanted my family to work by any means necessary. I didn't care about anything else. He was making it clear that he was nowhere near ready to build a family with me. I was providing for us all. He would pick up jobs but he never really gave any financial support. I felt like that was the best I could do and that no one would want me. I was a naive young teen with two little children.

As the relationship continued and time passed as well, I never got on birth control after having my daughter. Yeah, I know at this point, even if you wanted to have sympathy for me, you couldn't, because I messed around and got pregnant again, insanity (the seasoned generation calls this being fertile Myrtle). I kept making the same unwise choices but expected different results. I made up my mind early that this was an absolute no-go. I refused to even think too long about going through with it. I had to think fast once again. As I stated before, that is a gift of mine. I spoke with one of my close cousins about it. I told her I was too ashamed and there was no way I could go through with this. I called the Hope Clinic and explained my situation. I scheduled an appointment. At that time, they offered discounts for people who couldn't afford to pay full price. Even typing this makes me realize how crazy I was. I can't afford a $300 abortion but here I am constantly having unprotected sex which leads to more kids, (*shaking my head*).

I arrive and there are protesters outside. The ground of that place just didn't even feel or smell right to me. I knew I was dead wrong for even being there. I distinctly remember one lady who was there. She yelled to me, "Please don't kill your baby, I'll take it!" I almost shed tears right then and there. I knew they were right in trying to stop me. I don't judge others who decide to have an abortion. Every case is different. I am speaking about my own conviction. I knew that God did not desire that for my life. I felt it all through my body. I felt disgusted. It seems like the walk to get into the building took forever because I felt a crippling in my spirit as I heard the protesters attempt to stop me. The second-guessing started and I said to myself, "You know that this is wrong." But as always, I allowed myself to think about the task at hand and deal with the rest later. Going against the voice of God gets me in trouble every time.

I finally get inside and I'm all ready to go. A lady comes in to register me and to collect my portion of the payment. Over the phone, I told them I was able to pay $150, but between the days that the appointment was set and the time I went, I had to buy milk and diapers. I scraped up every dime I had to get as close as possible to the amount. I was, I believe, $12 short. She literally looked at me and said, "We can't do it if you don't have the full amount. You stated you had it over the phone." I'm thinking to myself like she's really going to act that way over $12? I was broke as a joke. I had to borrow the money so that I could proceed. I remember lying on the table as they performed the procedure; looking up to the sky and praying to God that everything goes well so that I can live to be with my children. I was in a daze for a moment as I listened to the doctors talk amongst each other. I knew that was just not a place I should've been. Thankfully everything went well and I felt like I dodged a major bullet in the physical realm, but my mind and emotions were jacked all the way up. I am so glad that I have always had a conscience to know when I was doing wrong. I never used my situation as an excuse to do what I knew I shouldn't. Even if I did something wrong and people knew, I would always say, "I know I was wrong," and that is not right. Just because I still choose to do it does not make it ok. God literally never took his hands off of me. Don't take signs, warnings, and exits for granted. God always provides a way of escape. Always!

That abortion happened early on in 2007. I thanked God for having grace on me and made a promise I knew, and He knew, I wouldn't keep. I said I would never get pregnant again and that I would stop having sex before marriage. I truly did desire in my heart to do the right thing. I saw that my life was headed down a path of destruction. I wanted to reverse this vicious cycle. In my mind, I had it planned that I would simply stop doing it. But, of course, this flesh is weak and it was not that easy just to cut it off. I was so used to this that it started to feel normal outside, but inside, I knew it was bad. Not even three months after having the abortion, I found out I was pregnant again. I was still being young and foolish at this point, but some would say irresponsible. I was having kids back-to-back before I was officially an adult, by a man who just abused me and wouldn't even take care of the ones we already had. Abortion was not an option at this point, so I guess I have no other choice but to get prepared. Yep, a single mom of three children all under the age of five. Whoever had anything to say, I didn't care. I wasn't going to argue, feel guilty, or allow anything to make me mentally challenged. This was my life and I was going to figure it out. I had the wrong attitude but I wanted to prepare myself for the criticism, so I put on this hard, tough facade. I was only fooling myself though. I was in my secret place with God, honestly begging Him to take the baby away. I felt like the child would be better off in heaven than on Earth with these kinds of parents. I would cry day and night in the tub and when I lay down at night. Life felt sucky for me. I felt like an addict who had no hope of breaking free and getting clean from his/her addiction. I didn't want to continue to be selfish to children who were so deserving of the world and more.

Months and months go by, and I realize God had other plans. He was not going to take my baby to heaven. Instead, I was going to just have to suck it up and prepare. I started to get bigger and, of course, it became obvious what was going on. Everyone knew and although I felt shame, it wasn't as bad as I thought it would be. I started to embrace being pregnant and bringing another kid into the world. I got excited and started to do everything to prepare. I got super excited when I found out I was having a handsome baby boy. My family was very supportive and was with me the entire process. They made sure I got to all of my doctor's appointments and that my other two children were taken care of. This time around, my pregnancy was high risk for different reasons, so I was at doctor's appointments more than the normal visits. It seemed as if the time from me finding out I was pregnant, to me actually getting ready to deliver, came pretty quickly. I felt a different kind of excitement. Due to my previous choice to have an abortion, I was extremely grateful in knowing that I would be able to not only have a healthy baby, but I was happy that this pregnancy was a little less stressful. I had the support around me and I felt like I wasn't hiding anything and things were smoother.

I went to my very last appointment before my due date on December 13, 2007. My sister-in-law was kind enough to take me and wait with me. I was at the visit for an ultrasound. Because of my high risk, they gave me weekly ultrasounds. When I get there, everything appears to be ok. I felt great and I can't say I had any complaints. The technician performed the ultrasound and had a shocking look on her face. I didn't really think too much about it.

28

She said, "Hold on, I'll be right back." She comes back in, but this time she has the doctor with her. The doctor asked me if I was there alone. I told her no and that my sister-in-law was with me. She told me she was going to get her from the waiting area and bring her in. Now at this point, I became worried. The doctors came back in and asked me when was the last time I felt the baby move. I told her, "The night before." I was excited and laughing while rubbing my belly because the baby was moving way more than normal that night. She looked at me for a second with a blank stare and said, "Well, the baby is dead." I was shocked. My sister-in-law began to cry. I couldn't even move. Like, there is no way. He was just moving not even 24 hours ago. The doctor showed me on the ultrasound that he was not moving and there was no heartbeat. She quickly began to talk about the next steps. She explained that I needed to be induced and have the baby just like I would a normal kid. How devastating is that?

My sister-in-law started making calls to the family as I prepared. I was numb. I just knew everything was ok. Immediately the spirit of guilt arose again. All kinds of thoughts went through my head. I thought to myself, you prayed for God to take him away, now look, you're unfit to be a parent. You killed your baby. I started to feel like trash. Yes, I did pray that prayer, but I repented and was ready to accept the choice that I had made. I was really excited to meet my baby boy. My family was excited; his siblings were excited. How could this be? God doesn't make mistakes. He is perfect in all of His ways.

I didn't have much time to process the situation. The family started to arrive and I was induced and waiting to deliver my handsome baby boy. I went into labor which seemed to me to be pretty fast. I remember there being a room full of people in the delivery room with me for support. I wanted the whole process to hurry up and be over with. I remember when Jordan (my son's name) came out, multiple people were in tears, specifically the delivery doctor. She was very young (maybe about 28 years old) and from Africa. She was balling crying as if it was her child. I tried to cover my face and look to the side. I was hoping and praying that the doctors were wrong. I was praying for him to start crying, but after so many minutes, I realized this was my reality. Jordan looked identical to my oldest son. I mean, it was scary to see. He was such a handsome baby. He just looked so peaceful and at rest. Turns out the cause of his death was that his umbilical cord had wrapped around his neck multiple times and so tightly that he had knots in there. That is what caused him to stop breathing. I tried to make sense of things, but I just couldn't. How could this be? I just literally felt him moving around last night. I couldn't hold him or even stare at him for too long. His dad held him in his arms for a while, just balling. I was trying to process everything and remain strong for my other kids. We were eventually able to go home, but this time leaving the hospital without a baby felt different. I felt like a huge piece of me was missing. I just couldn't fathom him being gone like that.

After we buried him a week later (thanks to my mom for footing the funeral bill) I started to really feel it. I tried to think of every possible thing I could to blame someone. I even tried to blame the hospital for not catching it beforehand at previous appointments. I had my mom get a malpractice lawyer. They checked into everything and got all of the medical records. They came back and said unfortunately they didn't find anything that the hospital had done wrong, so that was that. Now I had this visual of me being pregnant for nine months; preparing to have my baby at home with me, and the last thing I remember about him is that he was cold and blue and I never got to hear his cry.

It took me a while to be able to talk about him to anyone in a happy way. I never would even go visit his gravesite. I did get a tattoo with his name and birthday on my arm. It was my first and last tattoo (*lol*). Going to visit his gravesite or even acknowledging his birthday was always a hard thing for me, but in 2020 during the pandemic, I was just sitting and felt a strong urge to go see him. So, after 13 long years, I went to see him for the first time. I felt a heavy weight lift from me as I sat there and prayed and talked to God. I thought about how hard it is raising children in this world today; how hard it is to be a single mom of three, and I told God, "I thank You for Your will." My baby is in the safest place he could ever be. While I do miss him here on earth, God knew the plans He had for him before He formed him in my womb. Nothing I could have said or done could change His plans. I felt the guilt and shame lift from me. That was a big thing that took up a lot of mental space. I felt freedom in that area for the first time ever, but even years later, my children still ask about him. They remember him, and I pray that their hearts will be healed.

After that incident, I made sure I was not having any more children anytime soon and finally decided to get on birth control. At this point, I really understood that I needed to do something different with my life. I was failing, not a failure, but failing. The choices I'm continuing to make are just not smart at all. None of them makes sense. I had to make a change, and I needed to do that fast. The entire time I knew better. I grew up in church and had a mother who taught me the right things and ways to live. Although I didn't like the religious stuff, it taught me conviction and how to live a pleasing life for my Father. The crazy thing is that God has always spoken directly to me in many different ways. When I didn't even have the wisdom enough to recognize His voice, He was always with me. I could be in the middle of wrongdoing and He would speak, but like many of us do, I would override that still small voice.

So now, here I've had four kids with this man (I'm counting them all); still young, with no sense of direction for life. I said, "If I'm going to continue with this man, I'm going to at least do things God's way." So, I made it up in my mind that no matter what happens, I'm sticking it out to give my children a fair shot at having a family. They have seen and experienced too much for me to break them by breaking the family apart. Besides, it worked for my mom and dad. It wasn't the best relationship, but I was still able to be with both my parents. I decided I was going to take matters into my own hands and get him together. I started to invite him to church as a family with the kids. I thought in my mind he would hear the Word and it would hit him differently to where he would want to do right and be with his family. This is what happened when I went. The Word stuck with me no matter how I tried to do my own thing. Now at this time, I was still in high school, but I had this mindset as a young lady.

He graduated a few months before Jordan was born. I was so desperate for him. I would stay after school and do his work on the computer for him while he was out with other females. Had I not done this, he would not have graduated high school in time. I didn't care about any of that. I just wanted to be loved and to have my family work. It was really like I was raising another son. He started to come to church sometimes when I would ask. He was actually baptized after a while. That really sparked a different fire in me. It gave me hope. Now everything on the back end was still what it was; horrible, but the facades were continuing to be put on. I was always forcing and begging him to do things, whether it was church, family events, or anything that would bring unity between us. We went down this path for another two years.

"IF ANY MAN HAVE AN EAR, LET HIM HEAR."

REVELATION 13:9

4

GOD'S TRYING TO TELL ME SOMETHING

I finally was out of high school and wanted to do something with my life that would enable me to provide a good life for my children. I was able to get my first apartment when I was 19 years old. It was in the same townhome complex where my mom lived. My unit was just around the corner from my mother's. I was so happy to be able to be out of my mom's home and find some independence. I had always desired to be an adult and pay bills on my own. Now, I wish I could be a kid again (*laugh out loud*). Of course, he found out I was moving on my own and became this nice guy for a while. I understood that it was all game. He ended up moving into my place with me and things got ugly. He was a heavy drinker and smoker still, so he wanted to be able to do things like drink and smoke in the house. Smoke was just a deal breaker for me because he had asthma and so did my son. My son had it really bad. Well, although I was still living this way with him, I just did not desire to have my home contaminated in that way. He would leave a lot and come into the house at all hours of the night. He brought others there sometimes to just chill and relax against my wishes. I did make him help with bills but that was where I went wrong. He was never really supporting my children financially, but like I stated earlier, I'm going to do whatever it takes to make this thing work.

I stopped saying things to him. At this point, I believe this is where I agreed to be a revolving door and punching bag. The rage of a person who is under the influence is indescribable. Every time I spoke about anything, he would say he was leaving and to give him his money back from the bills. Now, of course, I wasn't able to do that. I was broke as a joke. So, I would have to kiss up to him because I knew I wasn't going to be able to give him the money. I was really suffering in silence. But what can I do? I just took the beating in every area. I would always try to understand his ways and would often ask what was wrong with him. He would always say it's me nagging too much or he could do what he wanted because he was a grown man. I was basically over so much, but it's just something about a little security that makes you overlook the bigger picture. I knew I should not have been involved and that I was asking God to fix a problem He never intended for me to have. I felt like a zombie and I was just existing for the sake of my children.

I was still very cautious about having more children. I just couldn't even stomach the thought of bringing another child into this world with him. But there was a time when he begged me to have another baby. Once again, there I go being naive, so I gave in. We both were working minimum-wage jobs, on food stamps and low-income housing. I knew this was not the best decision, but I said, "Whatever." In June 2009, I gave birth to my youngest child Jaleah. She was absolutely gorgeous and just brought a different joy to my life. It was like I had peace and happiness that I hadn't felt in a very long time. Don't get me wrong, I loved my other two children dearly, but I dealt with the guilt of them having to witness so much dysfunction that it was hard for me to be happy around them often. I felt like I was letting them down tremendously.

Things went well for a moment, but I knew God was constantly speaking to me. One day we got into a huge argument about him sleeping around with another woman. He punched me multiple times but this time it was one to the face as well, and I had a black eye. At this time, I was working in the nursing home as a CNA. I often did double shifts just to be able to pay bills. I did everything I could to try and make the mark go away, but nothing worked. I stayed in the house hiding for two weeks. My mom would help with the kids; getting them back and forth to school. When she would come over to drop them off and come in, I would hide in the closet. I would tell her that I was at work so she wouldn't expect to see me. One day she came and my car was parked right in front of the house. I told her that the job had paid for a cab because they didn't want me having to drive back and forth since I was helping out with extra shifts. It was the most embarrassing thing ever and I never felt right lying. He would lie in bed chilling, relaxing, and watching movies like nothing happened while I suffered. He would continue to disrespect me and even talk to women on the phone while he lay next to me. He would even talk about me to them and say how he was just there for his children. It was sickening. There was a window of time when I had my sister come live with me and her boyfriend would stay there sometimes as well. It was a little comfortable having them there, but also a lot was going on in the house. He would complain to me about people being there but would act cool in front of them. I never asked him for permission to have anyone there because everything was in my name and he was inconsistent with being there.

I started attending church even more than ever. He would criticize me and say that I was going to church more than I was spending quality time with family. I was on a hard-core search for freedom. I desired to be at church every time the doors were open. I was hoping my commitment to God was enough for him to get his act together. He would sometimes attend church with me but it was contingent upon him needing something from me. Whether it was a drink or to use my car afterward. When we would go, the pastor would preach a lot about hell and premarital sex. I already knew it was wrong, but it would hit differently, but I would leave and go do the same thing; expecting different results. I started asking God to

36

take away the feeling of wanting to be loved so badly that I was accepting anything. I knew the issues were much deeper than I realized. I was longing for the love I never received from my father. As far as feeling beautiful and worthy is concerned, I have never really experienced it. Now, I have three kids, and that bothers my self-esteem. There is no way any other man would want me and I am under 25. I would be looked at like a whore with no sense of direction in life. He would even tell me things like that when I would make comments about me leaving him and getting what I truly deserved. So those were thoughts that were added on top of me already feeling that way. I was told by others all the time how beautiful I was, but it never would register with me.

I would go through his phone and social media while he was sleeping and would be disgusted. There were all types of pictures, videos, and texts; just every woman's nightmare. He would be cheating with women just about everywhere he went. Work was the biggest issue. Imagine seeing these things. It's one thing to know what was going on but to see it was a whole different ballgame. He would be talking about me like I was the devil himself. I was warned so many times by many different people who loved me, even my pastor, that he was a hindrance to me, but I did just as others often did; ignored the warning. God can do anything, right? Can he change his heart? I mean he is coming to church. The Word is cutting him, I'm sure. I'm just not seeing the fruit of it yet. I thought to myself, people are just hating; they don't want to see me happy. Although, I was miserable. But these people cared a lot about me and I knew this.

One day we argued so badly because I was just so tired of the disrespect and abuse. I mean I was fed up. But it never stopped because he just wouldn't do right. I saw the behaviors of my children changing because of this relationship; him being in and out; the arguing and fighting. It affected my son the most as he started showing signs of anger. I knew this thing was more serious than I portrayed it to be, especially when my children would ask for him while he was on one of his missions and not being able to see their dad on a regular basis. I had to work more hours and could barely be home with my children. My sister had moved out at this point but thankfully my sister-in-law was with me and helped a lot with the kids. It just became so much. I couldn't handle it any longer. I wanted him to leave and he refused. He was talking about how he had paid bills and it's his apartment too. Now at this time, he hadn't been there for almost two months, so he was referring to the amount of money he had paid as a whole. I was not having it anymore. Normally I would make it work because I couldn't pay him back, but this time I stood my ground and told him I didn't have the money and I didn't care. He had to go. I admit I was just so tired and angry. I was in his face yelling at him. He didn't like the fact that I was that close to his face which is understandable. I will never justify my wrongs. Things became so heated that my neighbors called my mom and she came over. I, of course, was able to play things off. So, she had a real talk with us and was telling me how I was wrong for being in the relationship, living with him unmarried, etc. She let me know that as long as I was living that way outside of God's will, it would be trouble. Not one lie told there, but by this time he had already punched me in the face. Now, he stated that I either swung on him or hit him first, but I honestly do not remember that. The punch to my face initially didn't hurt honestly. The police were called as well and he left out of the back door before they arrived. I don't recall who called them but I know they came. I did give a report and told them I was fine and didn't want to press charges. This situation ended up being worse than I thought.

The next morning, I woke up with so much pain in my face. I also tried eating food and couldn't chew because my top and bottom teeth would not connect. I knew then something was wrong. I went to the ER and found out that my jaw was broken. As I said, the initial punch didn't hurt that bad, but it did send me into a daze. My sister-in-law told me that he hit me harder than I thought when it first happened. I thought she was exaggerating, but she wasn't at all. The doctors told me I needed to have surgery immediately to fix it. I didn't tell many people, but my mom knew. I went in for surgery and I was so scared because of how serious it was, and being out under anesthesia. The surgery went great, but my face looked horrible. I looked like Kanye after his car accident. I had to get a metal plate in my mouth permanently to fix the problem. My face was swollen and hurting for weeks. I couldn't even leave the house.

The doctors told me I was lucky because things could have been much worse. They reported this to the police department. At this point, things were out of my control. Because I did tell them initially after the incident that he had punched me, they had enough evidence to charge him. It was a state case, so this time I could not drop the charges. I remember the lady detective telling me how worthy I was and that I should never cover up for a man abusing me the way he did. She told me that she had been called to my home a few times, but I just didn't remember her. She said all of the right things and I had to agree with her. I was so mad at the way I looked that a part of me didn't care about him going to jail. That was another way of escape that God made for me.

They got the warrant for him to be arrested, caught him one day, and took him into custody. I felt bad because I thought that maybe I did say something to provoke him, also him telling me that I was the one who charged at him. Like I stated, I honestly do not remember that. My thoughts were, now I'm really making a mess of my family. Now with him being locked up, I knew there was no chance for any help with our kids. I tried everything I could to get the case to be dropped, but the state was not having it. Rightfully so. Like always, I was trying to figure out a way to help him and clean up the mess. I have a cousin who is an attorney and I immediately thought of calling her. She was able to take on the case and tried everything she could to help. My mom was even in on helping me to have him released and paying the fees. When I initially hired my cousin, he had been locked up for about three weeks. We were hoping that he would get out with me testifying that I didn't want to press charges. He would call from jail weekly to get the court updates. He was hoping as well that he would be able to get out soon. I made sure he had money on his books and was able to call me while he was there.

We had the final court hearing to see if he would be able to get out immediately. At that time, he had already served 90 days. Although my cousin did a great job, he was sentenced to nine months total, I believe. I spoke with him that entire week leading up to the final hearing. He was really hoping and believing that he would be released. He was even telling me how he was there reading the Bible and having Bible studies with other inmates. All of this, of course, gave me hope, and I was praying for him to be released, but God had other plans still. Because the state had picked up the case, he had to serve the time. I remember when I told him the outcome, he cried on the phone and kept saying, "OMG." I was hurt honestly, but there was peace that I had. I was able to be free for that period of time. I was able to reconstruct some areas in my life. I was able to recover from my broken jaw. I wouldn't worry about him. Although I had paid my cousin back, she was so patient with me when I couldn't make the payments I agreed to on time.

Truthfully, my face, and the way I looked, became another thing I was insecure about. Still, to this day, it bothers me. Oftentimes people tell me that they can't even see the difference in my face unless I point it out. It caused my face to be lopsided. I look in the mirror and I am so self-conscious about it. It almost reminds me of a person that has had a stroke. I hate it. I know a lot of it is because of the things I've gone through, but I think about how I would look when I become older. Imagine already being made fun of by the person you love and now having such an important physical feature messed with. On top of that, I was insecure about my teeth. They were crooked and I was ashamed to smile. My mom used to take us to the candy store as children and get credit to make sure we had all the goodies for school. That, of course, spilled over to my adult life. I love sweets but I soon noticed the damage it was doing to my mouth and body. When we would argue, he would often call me crooked teeth or say it looks like I've been chewing on bricks. So yes, my mind was being tormented in many ways after this. As I write this now, it's baffling how I was always thinking of others even when they did me wrong.

I had no business caring that much about him being behind bars. I am out here suffering in silence and raising three kids all by myself. I started taking my relationship with God seriously again. I just felt like He allowed him to be put away for those months so that He could provide a way of escape for me AGAIN. His plans and purposes for my life never changed. I just hadn't gotten in line yet. I wanted His will for my life more than ever, but that fear of the unknown crippled me so much. There was peace and hurt throughout this journey. I felt like I was so close to being free but I just wouldn't fully commit to God and let go. It was all in my head and I knew the thing to do was to just do it. But I couldn't. I was in my own way.

He was finally released from jail. Of course, I was there like always to get him and made sure he had everything he needed. I was just a tremendous support. There was no remorse or gratitude from him. He continued to blame me but I just brushed it off and changed the subject. The fighting didn't take long to resume. He got out of jail being the same way he was before. He would ditch me and the kids to go kick it with his family and friends. He couldn't immediately find a job so he started working with a guy from the neighborhood that had a construction business. I never knew how much money he was being paid because it was cash, so he would give me what he wanted when he wanted. He was released on probation and had to attend classes for anger management. He would make sure he was at the house on the days he had to be there. It was convenient for him because he knew I was going to make sure he got there on time. It wasn't far from my home. I became very frustrated at this time because I thought how could you go to jail for that amount of time and get out and nothing changes? I mean seriously, it's like you are worse than before.

I started becoming even more stern with speaking to him about helping with bills the right way. I have always been a hard worker, so I would work multiple jobs to do whatever it takes. He refused to help and would leave when it was time to pay bills. I decided that enough was enough. I went to the child support office and filed a claim for him to pay me. I didn't care about us being in the same household. I needed help with these babies. By the time the case was approved and placed, he had found a real job on top of his side hustle. I never told him that I filed, so when he saw the money being pulled from his check, it was a blowup. In his mind, he has been here helping me and providing for his children. But that was so far from the truth.

Things began to get uncontrollably bad. I started seeing some behaviors in my children that were not good; especially my son. He would become angry and hit his siblings when they upset him. He was also having trouble focusing in school. All of the children were happy when we were together as a family, but when the fights broke out, they would go hide. Neighbors were calling the police to my house which seemed like every day. I was so despondent in my heart and disappointed in myself. This relationship was not only affecting my life but also my children. All I could think was I was a failure. I prayed to God once again like never before. I told Him, "I know that I am living a life that is not exemplary." Whatever I needed to do to get my life right, I was ready. I wanted to get it right. I cried more than I ever have. I was so unhappy. I was miserable. I felt low, disgusted, ugly, unworthy, and like a waste of a human. I felt like God was tired of hearing me cry out and not obeying Him. He was tired of providing me with ways of escape while I continued to leave myself in the situation. I was on my own and had to figure this thing out. My family and friends loved me and were doing everything they could to help me. At the end of the day, it had to be a choice I made. No matter what anyone said or did, I had to realize this for myself.

"...FOR IT IS BETTER TO MARRY THAN TO BURN."

1 CORINTHIANS 7:9

44

5

BOY LET'S JUST GET MARRIED

At one point in my life, unfortunately, I quit praying and communicating with God. I deemed it a waste of time. So, I decided that when it came to my children's father, I would just be ready for whatever came my way. I allowed him to just do and say whatever. I just didn't have the strength to care anymore. I think he got too comfortable with me being so quiet that he became extremely wild. I can't even explain the feeling of not allowing yourself to care. But God never left me. He reminded me of this out of nowhere. One morning, I had just put my two older children on the bus for school. After that, he and I had sex. I kid you not, not even five minutes later, we heard banging on the door. It was the sheriff and the office manager for my apartment complex. I was being evicted. They said, "Come on, you have 15 minutes to get all of your stuff and get out." I called my mom crying and she was trying to calm me down.

Let me give you the backstory. As I stated before, while he was locked up, I was really drawing closer to God. I was experiencing God's hand in my life like never before. God was providing and making ways out of no way. It was remarkable. Before the manager who came to evict me took over the apartments, there was another manager who happened to be a Christian. She left right before he was released to take another position. She called me one day and said, "Regina, do you know that you have a huge credit on your rent account?" She said for over nine months I had been overpaying my rent. I had over $1,500 in credit. My rent was only $83 because I was in low-income housing, so I was so excited about that. I figured they would let me know when the credit ran out and it was time for me to start paying again. I believe that if the previous manager was still there she would have definitely let me know. I will take responsibility and say that I should've checked on it myself being an adult, instead of assuming. Lesson learned.

So, I was behind on my rent by about $1,000. I received a summons for court and that is how I found out. Now, I know $1,000 doesn't seem like a lot of money, but it was for me. I barely had ten dollars to my name. The court date came so fast; I believe within two weeks of me receiving the paperwork. Another level of stress added to me. There was no one I could think of at the time to go to for help. I wouldn't dare bother my family who already does so much for us. I didn't want to ask anyone because I have a man living with me and he should be the one helping me. But he was part of the reason I was in the jam. The judge gave me ten days to make the payment unless the manager agreed to more time, or I would have to leave. She agreed in the courtroom that she would give me more time. She stated that she would put it in writing for me. She never did. I called the office repeatedly and left her many messages. She never responded, so I assumed that the agreement we made was valid. Wrong again. She wasn't a nice woman and would always have a bad attitude when I would go in to speak to her. Many tenants complained about her but there was nothing we could do about it. I just wanted peace so I didn't pay any of that much attention. She had lied about coming to the agreement that she would give me more time and was avoiding me in every way that she could. So, when I got the knock on the door, I was shocked and scared. 15 minutes to pack an entire house up with no U-Haul or anything? I had to think fast.

My cousin was also living with me at this time, so I had to wake her up to leave as well. I called my brother-in-law to come help me. My oldest brother had a business that he worked for, so I knew that he had a truck that could fit most of my items in. I was trying to talk to the manager while they were evicting me, but she kept turning her head. I was furious and hurt. I don't know how I was able to get my things but I made it happen. I moved back in with my mom and some of my other siblings. She lived right around the corner on the same street where my children attended school. We somehow made it work. Now, my mom did not play the boyfriend-girlfriend thing, so he was not allowed to spend the night there. All I could think about was God was punishing me because I wasn't listening, but in reality, He was answering my prayers. The entire time I thought God was quiet, He had a plan. God loved me so much that He did whatever it took to get my attention time after time. I was just grateful that my children were not home to witness the chaos concerning the eviction.

He went back to live with his mom, but through all of that, nothing changed. I was still dealing with him and finding ways to be in his presence. No lessons learned here. By now, it was a soul tie that seemed impossible to break. We would do things together as a family and I was glad that my children were still able to see him. One night I was thinking to myself, I am still in the same boat. God was not pleased with me being in this relationship and not being married. I was going to church multiple times a week; reading the word of God which clearly speaks about premarital sex and how God is not pleased with it. Those were the only thoughts I cared about at the time. Knowing that I was being abused and treated poorly, I wanted to justify the relationship and wasn't quite ready to give up. I could talk a good game but I knew in my heart I wasn't ready to fully let go. I can't remember a time when we were able to get along for more than two days at a time. It was just always bad. I bit my tongue more for the sake of my children. I started to speak to him more and more about marriage. I kind of put fear into him as well, saying how we were being cursed because we were not living right and we would go to hell. Now mind you, I'm still living with my mom. He's with his family. And he was still sleeping around with multiple women. I just wanted my life to be ok for once. I wanted to prove that I had the power to live right and to be blessed, not realizing that I was making this relationship more important than God. I was idolizing it. I wanted a family so badly that I would continue to find ways to make it work the way I wanted and add God into the mix.

We came to a mutual agreement after several talks that we would go ahead and get married. We went to the courthouse one day to get the license. I knew deep down that there was no way I should even be considering this. As a little girl, I dreamed of having a man propose to me with all of my family and friends there. I wanted a nice wedding and to walk down the aisle. I wanted my marriage to be really special like I watched in the movies. We sought counsel from my pastor and first lady before getting married. They didn't know much about him other than when he would come to church sometimes and chat with them for a while after service. I know that my mom said that the pastor called her and asked if she thought it was ok for him to marry us and she gave the ok. I think my mom just wanted to see me live right and she was afraid for my soul, but she knew deep down that was not the man God had for me. She knew I was an adult and I would make my own decision no matter what.

We decided a few days after getting the license to get married. We texted family and friends to let them know that on Thursday evening we would be at the church to officially make this happen. I remember on our way there we saw some of his family members and told them to head to the church to witness it. I had my two best friends sign off on the license. Nothing felt right but I kept blowing it off. We had our close family and friends there to witness this. Nothing special, just a really small ceremony. After we said our vows, he started crying. He said that he couldn't believe that I still wanted him after all of the hell he had put me through. That was a wow moment for me. It showed me how I was so numb and good-hearted. In retrospect, he knew that he wasn't worthy of me. I don't say that arrogantly because I am not perfect, but he and others knew it. Why didn't I? It just revealed that I had something deep inside of me that caused me to feel like I was a garbage dump.

Honestly, I felt the pressure of sin lift off of me after we were officially married. In my mind, he is serious this time about doing right and being a family man. We are here now and finally doing things the way God designed them to be. It seemed like good things were just beginning to happen. There was a season where we got along really well. We were able to communicate the right way and be a good example for the children. He stopped going to his mom's house after church to spend time with our family. My mom would sometimes allow him to stay the night at her home with us. She made it clear that since we were married it didn't bother her for him to be there. The apartment was really small though and already crowded. I knew I needed to start looking for another apartment. Of course, I was worried because of the eviction. I looked at several places but that was holding me back from getting anything. So, I had to stay with my mom the entire first year and a half that we were married.

I prayed daily for God to give me a second chance to be able to get a place for me and my family. God answered like He always did. It was not an easy process but the owner of the apartments took a chance on me and allowed me to move in. Coincidentally, it was a block away on the exact same street as the apartment I was evicted from. He was very clear that he was giving me a chance and he didn't want me to take that for granted. He stated he didn't care who I allowed to move with me or anything. He just didn't want me to cause any problems. He moved me right next to his mom. And his granddaughter lived on the right of me. I loved the apartment so much. We had three bedrooms and two and a half bathrooms. He stated that he didn't even care if I moved unauthorized tenants in. He just didn't want drama in his place. I was so grateful and did everything to try and keep the peace. But nothing worked. He met new friends out in the complex and started to do more of the hanging out and drinking. I came to the conclusion that he would continue to be who he was.

I needed to decide what I wanted for the future of my children. I made up my mind to go to nursing school. I always desired to be a nurse but with life happening, I just didn't believe I had the time or ability to do it. But I took a chance. I failed the entrance exam about eight times before finally having a shot at being accepted. I went through the process and was accepted after a few months. The program was an accelerated one and it was two years crammed into one. I was determined to make it through. I just wanted a better life for myself and my children. I wanted to prove to myself that I was worthy and that I was somebody. I thought that having a degree or career made me somebody. I never wanted to be the woman who lived in poverty all of her life and used government assistance to take care of my children. School was no joke. It was an extremely hard program, and dealing with a cheating lying husband affected me so badly mentally. I had great support all around me, but mentally I couldn't stay focused. My husband would be there to help with the children while I studied. I made it through classes literally by a thread.

After a few months of me being in school, he met a woman at his job and started to have a real affair. It was different because he spent lots of time with her and would leave for longer stints of time than before. I found out who the woman was and I confronted her about sleeping with a married man. She said that she didn't care that he was married and even less about my feelings and continued taunting me. I felt highly disrespected. He tried to end things with her, at least that's what he told me, but she started playing on my phone saying that she was pregnant. It seemed like the attacks were coming back-to-back. He ended up going back to her. This time he stayed away for four months. Due to this unwarranted entanglement, I didn't even want to continue with school because I was so stressed. I remember I became very sick and dizzy. I was in and out of the ER for a week. I never really had health issues, but I was so stressed that I began to have seizures. I was just existing, but I made a decision that I was going to live for my children.

Not too long after I became sick, the engine in my jeep went out. That was my only means of transportation and, of course, I didn't have money to get that repaired. My oldest brother paid for the engine to be repaired. I was beyond grateful. My support system is top-tier. So, I was able to continue with school and work, all while my husband was seemingly living his best life with another woman. My car was fine for a few months; I believe about two. One day, as I was driving home from picking the children up from school, a man flagged me down and told me there was a fire under my car and I needed to get out. I was so scared and moved faster than I ever had before. I grabbed my purse and my children and we ran, and not even ten seconds later my car exploded right in front of our eyes. I was devastated. I couldn't believe it. I was so grateful we were not harmed, but now what?

Because of me being a single parent at the time and being in school, I did not have any car insurance. It was a total loss. I felt like there was just a dark cloud and curse over my life. I was fighting with really no strength. Not long after, I failed out of nursing school. I was six points short of what I needed to make it to the last trimester. All hope just seemed to be lost for me. I knew I didn't have the time to focus the way I needed to in order to have success. I decided to just continue to work as a CNA and provide for the children the best way that I could. God's plan never fails so I knew He was working things out for me. I prayed harder than I had ever done before. I fasted more than ever and went to every church service that was available multiple days a week. Eventually, he came home and I really couldn't even fight with him anymore. I just went along with whatever. He even skipped a month of paying his portion of the bills because he said he loaned his mom money. I made a statement about that not being ok and he cursed me out and told me to never say anything about what he does for his mom. Nothing was new under the sun. The young lady that he left and was involved with for that long period of time reached out to me and was very apologetic and kind of told me some things she had experienced as a child - watching her father cheat on her mom - and she understood where I was coming from when I spoke to her about the effect it had on my children. She also stated that she felt like some bad things that were happening in her life were karma from being involved with my husband. I can rock with that and I did forgive her.

I started to plan more date nights and family time to work on staying positive and to grow and forgive. I didn't want to become bitter and angry so I had to do things to keep my spirit right. I wanted to love and to feel loved. I didn't mind constantly being in denial for the instant gratification that came with having a good time with my family. Once my husband started to stay home more consistently, although still cheating, I wanted to be able to do some bigger things as far as having greater experiences. My older sister and her then-husband were always traveling and getting away. They invited us on a trip with them to take a cruise. I was super excited because we had never been out of town, let alone on a cruise. Of course, anything extra outside of bills, I had to pay for. I didn't mind. I was looking forward to being able to get away from our parenting and work for a few days. The trip was about $800; which I worked extra hours to be able to pay for. Hard work never scared me. The time came for us to travel. I had everything set up as far as things we needed and childcare for the children. My husband was not used to life outside of the hood, so I thought this was going to be super special.

A few days before we were to leave, he started an argument with me about something I can't even remember. He then stated that he wasn't going on the trip and left. Hold up - was all I could think. I have worked overtime and set things in order for the children, and you do this? I said nothing wrong to him. I had not mentioned anything about other women, his drinking, or anything. I wanted this to be a real good time. He left and stood on business. My sister was still telling me that I should go alone because I had paid and couldn't get the money back. I was contemplating going but decided not to go because I wasn't in the mood and my spirit was crushed. $800 went down the toilet. This made me hate everything about the nice me. I didn't want to ever do anything else nice for him because I was tired of being disrespected. No matter what I did, it seemed like I continued to get the short end of the stick. I was being abused in every way possible. Why do I want to be loved so badly that I keep hurting myself hoping for this man to change?

I
RELEASE
SHAME.
IT DOES
NOT
BELONG
HERE WITH
MY HEART.

6

A CAR CAN'T BUY YOU LOVE

A few years went by and things were good for a while. I was in a good head space. The fighting was not as bad, because like I mentioned before, I just didn't care. The physical abuse was not as bad, but the verbal and emotional abuse was still there. I had learned to cope with it. I am a very attentive and compassionate person. I pay attention to others when they express themselves and talk about certain things they desire. He always talked about an old-school car called a Cutlass. He had issues getting his driver's license because of some tickets and other issues, but he always would drive like he was legit. I wanted to do something nice to make him smile and know that he was worthy. I asked my brother-in-law who specializes in cars, especially old schools, to assist me in finding something for him as a Valentine's Day/you are worthy gift. I had received my income tax return and had extra money to spend. He found the perfect Cutlass for $1,800 with low miles, and very clean.

I planned the perfect setup to gift him the vehicle. He had absolutely no idea. I had butterflies thinking about how excited he would be and how I was the one that was going to make him smile like he hadn't done in a while. I was buying him his very first vehicle. We headed out for dinner on Valentine's Day. My brother-in-law had come to my home in the vehicle. I tricked my husband and told him, "My mom wanted to assist you and do our laundry." I had him take the basket of clothes to the car and told him my brother-in-law was out there to get them for my mom. When he got outside, he didn't recognize the car so I said, "Here, put them

55

in your car." He was confused and thought I was being funny. Then he said loudly with a huge Kool-Aid smile, "This ain't my car." And my brother-in-law handed him the keys. He was so excited. I believe that was the first time I had ever seen him that excited. My brother-in-law had the title and asked before we pulled off if I wanted to sign it. I didn't want my husband feeling like I was trying to control his gift so I said, "Nah, I'll wait until we get back. Give it to him to put up." So, my husband took the title in the house and came back out to leave. This was one of the first times I heard God speak to me and say sign the title, but I disobeyed.

We finally headed to dinner to enjoy the night. We drove my car because the Cutlass wasn't registered or insured yet. As we were driving, he had his music playing on the speaker. He asked me to change a song so I grabbed his phone. Something told me to go through it. I was sick to my stomach after discovering what I saw. He was cheating with multiple women. Some I knew from high school and some that he worked with. Once again, I felt so foolish. I couldn't believe I allowed myself to believe things were different. While he was driving, I confronted him about it and, of course, he flipped the script. He started to curse at me and told me I had no business going through his phone and how he was done with me. He turned the car around and said he was going home and leaving. I felt so used. Seriously? I had just done a huge thing by purchasing him a vehicle and now he is using me confronting him as an excuse to leave again. I thought to myself, Regina, if you would've just not said anything, things would've been peaceful. It was my fault again.

While driving back home, all I could think about was the title and how I didn't sign it. I knew he was going to go home and try to leave with the car. That's absolutely what he did. He ran into the house, signed the title, packed his bags, and left. I tried stopping him but that only turned into him being so violent that I just

56

called the police. They told me there was nothing they could do because the title was signed. I would have to go to court. I was furious. I got into my car and chased him in the Cutlass. Now looking back on it, that was extremely dangerous. I caught up to him at one point and even rammed into his car. I chased him from St. Louis, Missouri to East St. Louis. He was eventually able to get away. I tell you, a broken heart not handled correctly can have you making emotional decisions that can cause much damage.

I spent the next few days calling the courts to see what I needed to do to get my vehicle back from him. There weren't many options. I decided that I was going to just let God deal with him, and He did just that. He didn't have the vehicle very long before God showed up. He had a best friend that he allowed to drive the car. He was pulled over by the police because the car was not registered correctly and it was impounded. Now, my husband couldn't afford to get it out so it eventually went to the auction to be sold. He went to my pastor and a few of my close family and friends asking to borrow money to get it out, but no one could help him. God worked that thing out just the way He designed it, even though I was disobedient by not listening and signing the title. Although I lost $1,800, he lost more than I did and God reminded me that He fights for me. My husband was in a low place again because he messed up such a good gift.

He came back home about a month after losing his vehicle. I was doing my normal mother and wifely duties, but this time, something with him was different. It seemed like he was meaner or doing something other than drinking alcohol. I would become so frustrated with him and the way he was treating his family that I would say some harsh things. I am far from perfect and I admit that. I felt like the only way that I could fight him was with my words. He was a physically strong man, especially while drunk. I can't beat you up, but I can make you hurt with my words. Foolish way of thinking, but that was how I thought back then. I know this was another reason why I stuck around because I felt the guilt of knowing I wasn't perfect and had many flaws. I apologized to him and asked God to help me to correct that flaw of mine. I remember praying and asking God to do whatever it took to get his attention. I wanted him to just do right for once in his life. My children were hurting, I was hurting, and life was horrible for me. I thought something's got to give. I was never the woman who would run from adversity. I never cheated and never entertained other men while I was married or prior. When I started getting serious with him, he was the only man I dealt with. Men would always come and attempt to date me, but I was never going to open those doors.

My husband left home again to stay at his father's house in East St. Louis. He was gone at this time for about three months. He would pop in on us but that's pretty much it. One Friday, after leaving my children's school performance, we were in the store buying them coloring books so we could go around the corner to my mom's house. I got a call from an unknown number. It was a doctor from SLU Hospital in St Louis informing me that my husband had been shot. She said that he was ok and was going into surgery. He asked the paramedics to call me. I panicked and told my kids, "We have to go. Your daddy got shot." We ran out of the store and thankfully I made it to my mom's house to drop the kids off as my sister and father were leaving. I started making calls as I rushed to the hospital. I had peace on the inside of me, but on the outside, I was feeling scared. It seems like it took hours to get to the hospital although I was driving super fast. When I arrived my sister and brother-in-law pulled up at the same time. I was happy they were there because his family and I didn't speak much. He had planted a lot of bad seeds about me which caused tension (thank God we are all cool now).

We waited a while before the doctor came out with the report. She asked where his wife was. He was out of surgery and doing well. He was shot four times, but he was wearing a jumpsuit that I believe saved his life. He asked to see me. Now in my mind, I'm thankful that he was ok, but also feeling some type of way. Now you want your wife? The same wife you left months ago to be alone with your three children? I didn't care though. I know that my vows meant something to me. My commitment to honor God meant something to me as well. He was released from the hospital a few days later. I knew that God had answered my prayers. Yeah, this is going to be it. Now he's really about to get his act together. God spared his life and I'm sure he was terrified. Nope, while leaving the hospital he asked me to take him to get beer. I argued with him because how are you thinking about alcohol and you can barely walk? One of the places he was shot was in his stomach. It was stitched up and taped. He was furious that I wouldn't do it so I just gave in and took him. It was a sad sight watching him go into the liquor store holding his bloody stomach to get beer.

He came home with me and I cared for him until he was well enough to take care of himself. It was extra stressful. I had to help him with bathing, walking, and changing his patches for a few weeks. But I didn't complain. My children still had their father and my husband was alive, which is all that mattered. He attended church with me when he was able to move around just a bit more comfortably. Eventually, he was well enough to be right back in the same environment and started going backward. He wasn't taking anything seriously.

The drinking intensified. One day he left in my car while I was asleep. One of the females he was dealing with called and told me to keep my keys because he kept popping up in my car at her house. I was heated. Often, he would take my car keys while I was asleep and come back the next day. This time when he came

59

home, he was so drunk I couldn't stand to see it. I confronted him about what the young lady told me about him coming to her home in my vehicle. Just no respect for me at all. He was so drunk it made no sense. He began to abuse me and call me names. My kids tried to get him off of me, but they couldn't. We were standing at the top of the step to my apartment. My neighbor, who is the owner's granddaughter, knocked on my door and asked if I was ok. She said she had called the police and they were on the way. My children were crying and screaming. My neighbor was speaking to him and telling him he was wrong and a coward for beating me. I felt so foolish and embarrassed. The police came and he called his mom to pick him up. I remember just hugging my children and apologizing to them for allowing them to be in such a messed-up situation. I see now how people just go through life wanting to successfully make it through the day because it becomes so miserable. I started to seek counsel from other church members. They would tell me things like, "Continue to pray for him that God would save him. The sanctified wife sanctifies the husband. Don't give up. God hates divorce. He will save him. You just need to continue to fight and be the light." I did everything that I knew to do.

MY
NEEDS
ARE
IMPORTANT.

7

A LEOPARD DOESN'T LOSE ITS SPOTS

I wanted a fresh new start. I thought of ways to get us away from the same environments and to have better opportunities for my children. The school they attended was ok, but it also caused a lot of stress for my son because he had to deal with kids who were not always the nicest. I was grateful, but more was out there. One day I was driving to work and I passed some townhomes that were visible from the highway. I said out of faith, "I'm going to move over there." The location seemed to be perfect. A lot of the stores I shopped at were conveniently located there and the area seemed very quiet and nice. I tried my best to drive directly to the townhomes, but the way the streets were laid out, I couldn't find them. I could see the townhomes from the highway, but they weren't that easy to find. Days went by and I was doing all the research I could to find the name of the townhomes. No luck.

I went to work one day and was just having a casual conversation with one of my charge nurses and she stated that she had moved to Kirkwood, Missouri a while back. I asked her if they were the townhomes you could see right off of the highway and explained to her that I had been searching for them and wanted to move there. She gave me the information to call and let the manager know that I was interested. I stood there shocked and amazed. This girl just blessed me with the information I had been praying for. I felt good; like a breakthrough was coming. I didn't know the price of the place or anything. I didn't care. I just knew that I wanted better. I called the office and the manager told me that she would put me on the waitlist. She said that the list was so

62

long and I would remain there anywhere from three to four years. I was crushed in my spirit for a moment because I had gotten so excited only to hear that. Now I knew that I couldn't afford much rent. We were on income-based housing and didn't make much money. It was faith that made me call and make the move. I continued to trust God, pray, and fast. I knew eventually something would come up for us. I searched a lot for places to move but nothing was working in my favor.

One day I was home just relaxing and God told me to start packing as if I had the keys to my place and everything. I didn't have a clue about where we were going. All I knew was that I had prayed and asked God to bless me to be able to move before my lease was due for renewal. I kid you not, I got boxes and just started packing. I made a status on Facebook that said, "I just packed my boxes and have no clue where I'm going, but I trust God." Three days after making that post, I got a phone call. It was the manager of the townhomes in Kirkwood, Missouri. She said, "Regina, your name came up on the list and we have a place available for you." I am getting teary-eyed writing this right now. God did that for me. It came at a moment when I needed it the most. It was God reminding me that He is with me always. I was so happy. Right now, I am reminded of that moment and I am joyful. God is perfect. A list I thought I would be on for years, I wasn't even on it for three months. Favor ain't fair. He moved swiftly because I obeyed. My children were so excited to move into the new space. The area was amazing and the school district was #2 in the entire state. My husband worked at Five Guys Burgers and Fries in Kirkwood prior to us moving, so it made things super convenient for him. His job was about seven minutes away, and with him not having a car, he was able to walk.

For a moment, there was freedom. By us moving so far away, many of his friends and family would never come there to hang out. Most were scared to be in the area because of the police. The place was perfect and I started to hope again. He started to meet new friends out in the area and I was ok with them. Of course, it's not hard to become friends with neighbors. I felt a little comfort in knowing I didn't have to worry about all of the attacks that came from his family and friends who were closer in distance to our old place. I was ok and at peace for a moment, but he began having affairs with the women on his job. Ridiculous right? Five Guys...I thought I was safe, but obviously, there were five guys and some gals working there as well (*laugh out loud*). I went through his phone after obviously knowing he was hiding something. He began to sleep with his phone in his underwear or tucked under his belly. I was doing my best to stay focused and be a good person/parent. I saw so many disgusting texts and videos every time I searched his phone. It caused me to have major self-esteem issues. But it all goes back to choosing your battles wisely. I knew that confronting him would just lead to more and more chaos, and on top of the chaos, he would always justify his wrong; basically, spitting in my face and saying, "I will be who I am. Deal with it."

I would cry at night so much. Every time I found out who the woman was that he was cheating with, I would find her on social media and stalk her page. I would go through her pictures and begin to compare myself to her. I would feed my mind thoughts that had no business being there. I would also try to talk like them to him and use the same nicknames for him that they used. I had a very hard time speaking the words baby or bae to my husband. I never understood why, but I believe it had a lot to do with the way I grew up; not having that strong emotional or verbal communication about love. My mom showed love but never really verbally expressed it. I would do things to always show my husband that I loved him even if I didn't say it a whole lot. I didn't know what was wrong with me. I understood that I could nag at times and say harsh things, but so did he. I wasn't the perfect woman but I did everything to make sure the family was good. I never cheated and never gave in to the temptation that I faced. It was a losing battle because he had opened himself up to so many things with other women. Sex became a thing I wish I didn't have to do. I became so disgusted and felt like I wasn't good enough in the bedroom, especially with him constantly leaving and cheating. I felt like I was becoming an old woman faster than I should have. There would be women who knew he was married and it seemed like that made them go harder to have him. They would buy him things, give him money, and let him borrow their cars. I felt like the more I prayed and fasted, the greater the attacks became. I just wanted my family to work. I was desperate for my children to experience firsthand what a good marriage and family felt like. I knew that there had already been lots of damage done to them, but they loved their parents no matter what and loved the good moments that we shared.

Location will never change a person. In my mind, the move was a step toward a healthier marriage. Unreasonable to think that way I know. I would often ask him why he cheated and drank the way he did, but he would always deny everything and say that I was tripping or judging him. He said nothing was wrong with him and that I assumed things. As far as the beers he drank per day, he would say they weren't that many. I learned that he was selling weed out of my house to some people who lived in my neighborhood outside of my complex. That caused an argument and his position was that he was paying half of the bills so he could do whatever he wanted. He also was upset because he said that he was already paying child support and I was also making him pay bills. He would try to convince me to lift the order since he was back home, but I never would do it. The order was only for $371 for three children; which was not much at all. He justified not paying his half of the bills by using that story. Our household bills were way more than that per month and he was not consistent enough with being around.

Around 2016, things just became so bad for me. The alcohol abuse was just unbelievable. I began to recognize that I had to do something fast. I found out that he was dealing with one of the women from his past. He would just pick so many fights with me daily for no reason. He even began having phone conversations for hours with this young lady while he slept on the couch. Things had become so bad that we couldn't even sleep in the same bed. I was ok with that because I was so turned off that I refused to sleep with him again. It's one thing to say you are tired of certain behaviors, but it's different when you truly make up your mind that you're tired and say enough is enough. I began to see myself desperate for attention; desperate for compliments. I just wanted to hear that I was beautiful and loved. It seemed like I was never hearing it and I stopped believing that I was any of those things. I did work as much as I could just to stay away from him at home. I was sad about leaving my children but I knew the ship was not going to move if I didn't go make it happen. Besides, being away from him was my peaceful place. Just to be able to be out in the normal world, but also making money, made me feel amazing. I felt I had no identity besides being a wife to my husband and a mother to my children. My friends were always there but, of course, everyone had their own life and family, so we couldn't hang out as much.

One day I was out at a church service and my husband was home alone with our children. I wanted to make a stop at a store before going home, but something told me to head straight home. As I entered my home, I heard my children upstairs screaming. I quickly ran up the stairs to see what was going on. I opened the door to my daughter's room and my husband was standing there drunk with a belt. He had my oldest two children bent over getting ready to whoop them. I quickly pushed him away and grabbed the belt. He became so mad and started cursing me out. He was saying things like I was wrong because those were his children and that he could punish them. He said that I never punish them and that is why they were pushovers. He was so drunk he could barely stand up. He then began to insult my children and once again threatened to leave. This is the time when he told my daughter who was initially given up for adoption that I didn't want her and that I gave her away to White people as a baby. That crushed my spirit so badly that I lied and told her he was not being truthful. He even said he had pictures to show her. Just evil. He'd say anything to hurt me.

I grabbed my children and hugged them so tightly. I was so grateful that God had directed me to head home when I did, but I also felt so bad for leaving them home alone with him. I know that sounds crazy because he is their father but he was just not fit to be responsible for them at the time. The argument that night was one of the longest ones we've ever had. It lasted for hours. It was late that night but he assured me that he would be gone the next day. It was so mentally draining and all I could think about was my children and how this was impacting them emotionally and their future overall. I understood the importance of protecting your children, especially in the mind. I have always fought the battle of the mind. I realize that if your mind is attacked in certain ways, it can cripple your entire life. I knew this was horrible for my children to witness. I had to do something.

The intimacy between us was pretty much non-existent. Yes, I would periodically have sex with him but there were no real feelings there. I just couldn't take it anymore. He had a brother who was released from prison after serving many years whom he began to hang out with a lot. I was happy that he was able to form a bond with him because he had gone away while my husband was very young. They spent lots and lots of time together so my husband would be gone the majority of the time unless he had to work. His brother had also started a relationship with a young lady so he was living his life and making himself happy. One day my husband and I argued because I had been asking him to assist me with cleaning the house and he just refused to. I knew something was up and he was planning to possibly leave because he began to act weird. He went to sit on the front porch but he didn't realize that I had seen him pack some clothes. I went to the porch to confront him but he acted as if he didn't hear me.

There was a lockbox in our bedroom where I kept money for emergencies. Something told me to go and check that box. He had stolen my money from there. By the time I made it back down the steps and opened the front door, he was gone. I could see the outside of the gate from my home and saw this black car leaving. I quickly grabbed my keys, rushed out of the complex, and followed the car. I had on one shoe and I'm pretty sure I was speeding like crazy. I was so mad. How could he do this? It was not the first time that he had stolen money from me. I could see if I was trying to stop him from leaving but none of that was taking place. I was able to catch up to the car and the young lady who was driving stopped. He knew the area we lived in was no joke. If there was any form of drama or disturbance of the peace, the police would be called and they would arrive quickly. We were right in the back of Lowe's and there were employees working outside. The occupants of the car included his brother's girlfriend who was the driver, her friend who was the front seat passenger, my husband and his brother who were in the back seat, and a young lady who sat in the middle of them. When I opened the back door, the young lady gave me a look I will never forget. The guilt was written all over her face. I knew then that my husband was sleeping with her. At

68

that point I didn't care, I just wanted my money. I asked him for my money and he refused to give it to me. He had a backpack so I grabbed it from his lap, got in my car, and left.

I began to cry as I pulled off to go back home. I said, "God, this is just not it anymore. I need You to force my hand to let this go. I don't know how at this point. I can't even see past what I am seeing now. HELP!" I began to have conversations with his mom and she confirmed everything about the young lady. He was indeed dealing with her. He had been involved with her for a few months. When he came back home about a week later, I began to investigate for myself. I didn't need to do much on my own because the young lady did something I never experienced before with anyone my husband cheated with. She would call and text my phone and tell me everything that they had done, all of the bad things he would say about me, and she also let me know that she wasn't going anywhere. She was a few years older than him as well. I was being tormented mentally like never before. I seriously began to worry about my safety physically, because I realized this young lady was not normal, and sexually, because of the stories I heard about her dealings with other men and I didn't want to get an STD. She would post pictures of them on Facebook and sometimes even go live and show his face. I understand that I didn't have to go and look at these things, but back then I was not as mature as I am now, and he was my husband.

God started to speak to me about this situation like never before. I started to feel my heart slowly drifting away from him. One night we argued because he had too many guys at my house sitting on the front porch just chilling. I got so fed up that I addressed him while they were sitting on the porch. I expressed I wasn't okay with that, especially because I knew that some of them were drug dealers. Now looking back, I don't think that was wise for me to do, but I was sick of it. He came into the house after they had left and all hell broke loose. He was so drunk and so mad. He began to put his hands on me in a way I never experienced. He got me into the bathroom, locked the door, and began to choke me. My children were outside the door screaming and crying. I had no strength. His eyes were so red. It was the most evil thing I had ever seen. I thought he was going to kill me. I'll never forget that. My oldest daughter became so afraid that she called the police and my mom. The police came and I refused to lie. He left that night.

The next day I went to file for a restraining order, but that didn't last very long. Looking at my children's faces, I knew this was it for me. No more can I make excuses for this type of behavior. This man is going to end up killing me. It's not worth it. This was God answering my prayers. On July 6, 2017, I went to file for a divorce. I had no idea what I was doing and was afraid. Yes, after the choking incident, he was able to come back home because, unfortunately, he was on the lease so I couldn't kick him out. He knew that I had filed but tried to convince me not to continue with it.

FINISHING TOUCH

IT'S FINE TO ASK FOR HELP AND SUPPORT.

8

YOU GOT SERVED

I remember the day when he was served. I had just dropped him off at work and had gone across the street to the gas station. He ran back over to me and said, "Take these home." He explained that he laughed at the man who served him and said to him, "Let me go give these to my wife so she can take them home." I knew then that he didn't take it seriously. I became really worried about him because of the drinking. I had asked him for months to go to the doctor to get a check-up. He was agreeing with everything because he didn't want me to divorce him. We went and they checked him out and everything came back normal. The doctor told him that he was ok now but on the route that he was going with drinking, he was going to end up killing himself if he didn't stop. He looked at me laughing and said, "I told you nothing is wrong with me." He also laughed at the doctor as she was explaining to him the seriousness of his alcohol usage. I knew God was setting me up and strengthening me. Another agreement he made was that he would stop drinking alcohol and that he would do anything to keep his family. And it seemed for a moment he had stopped. He was not buying beers and was coming home every day straight from work; not picking fights. I thought, the prayers really are working now.

One day, I noticed that he was going in and out of the bathroom. He had gone in multiple times in just a few minutes. He has never done this. So, I went in after him and looked under the sink and discovered that he was hiding the beer there and going in there to drink it. It was horrible. I knew the decision I was making was the right one. I finally received our court date for November 30, 2017. I never expected that we would get a date that soon. I became very nervous and sick. So many thoughts came to mind. How am I going to make it being a single mom of three children? How am I going to survive on my own when I am barely making it with him? No man is going to be interested in me with three children. I battled mentally for a while with these thoughts. I became very uncomfortable with life. I was just taking things day by day, but the weight of the divorce was weighing on me. I started to evaluate things about myself that could have possibly triggered some of his behaviors. I knew sometimes I wasn't the nicest with my words. I also know I would sometimes nag about things. None of it was intentional but the frustration that came with the relationship caused me to be that way. I wanted to be so sure that I was making the right decision and that I did what was necessary to right my wrongs.

I had a conversation with him and told him to write things down that I could do better, or things that he would like me to stop doing that were not pleasing to him. I made sure I checked everything off of the list; the emotional, physical, and sexual. I became uncomfortable with a lot of it because I was learning new ways to be, but I knew it would be worth it. First, for my conscience, and then for my marriage. I would be able to say I truly did give this thing my all. I remember planning a romantic night at home for us. I took some stripper classes. Don't judge me (*laugh out loud*). I bought a pole for the house and set it up to dance for him. I wanted to impress my husband. I had everything all nicely set up and ready to go. I told him that we were having a date night. He still chose to go out and party. He came home and I was super excited to perform and have a great night together. He walked in the door throwing up and went right upstairs and went to bed. I was devastated. I had worked so hard to get out of myself and to think of him in a way that I never did before. I paid money for classes and that took me way out of my comfort zone, and for him to brush me off after telling him that I had something special planned just made me sick.

None of the things that I tried worked. I found out that he was still sleeping around. He would get mad about me not being willing to use the pole I bought for him in the bedroom. I just couldn't bring myself to do it. Mentally it was tough to break through the emotions that I felt initially when he first walked into the house intoxicated. It was too much. Not only that, but he had gotten heavily involved with the young lady he hooked up with through his brother. I started to feel disgusted like never before. I learned that she was a very promiscuous young lady and was known for being dangerous. I started to worry about diseases and just being safe in general. The harassment became greater. She called me one day playing on my phone; telling me how she had sex with him; how he told her he was only with me for the kids, and she even went on to say that she had sex with him in my bed and told me how things looked in my house. Now at this point, the damage was so deep within me that I couldn't react. My tears became silent.

I just wanted to live again. When I realized that he was not going to change and that he would stay involved with that young lady, I had a mind shift. I said to myself, "This man is bringing you much more harm and danger than you know." I decided that I was not going to have sex with him anymore. I didn't care about what he did or said. His statement to me that I'm not supposed to deprive him of sex because that would make him cheat meant nothing. I was not going to continue to put my body at risk for anything damaging. I know that he was never one to use protection when he cheated. Enough was enough. I continued to deal with him for the kids. I was selfish toward myself and didn't care about what he did. I still needed him around for the kids. He would always tell me that he was not going to go to court when it was time for the divorce. He said that we were the family that he created and that they would have to find him before he showed up to finalize things.

I picked up more hours at work while I waited to go to court. I knew that if I was going to go through with this process I would need to make as much money as possible for me and my children. I prayed every day and some days I couldn't speak but God heard my silent tears. The closer it got to the date the more nervous I became. I began to question everything and tried to make it all make sense. I talked to everyone I could think of. There were mixed opinions. Some felt like I should stay and trust God and others thought I should let it go and trust God to sustain me and my children. He also started to be on me more and tried to talk me out of going through with things. He would text me all day while at work trying to convince me not to do it. He said he would do whatever to make things right with us. He showed me where he had blocked the young lady he was with and stayed home every day. He did nothing outside of working and being with us.

I caved in a little bit, well, a lot. It was time for me to renew my lease in the townhomes we lived in. It was due in September. Initially, I didn't plan to have him on the lease so he didn't need to fill out any paperwork, but with him convincing me to give him another chance, I allowed him to go into the leasing office with me to do his portion of the paperwork. Once he signed his portion and I signed mine, I had no authority to have him removed from the lease, but I believed it could be different this time, especially with him knowing I was serious because I actually filed paperwork. There were about ten days left before my court date. I was at work ready to let the court date pass and continue in the marriage. I called the court and asked what would happen if

I pushed the court date back some. They told me that I would have to wait until the following year to get a new date because the dates were filled due to the holiday season. I told the clerk I was considering it and would give her a call back. I kid you not, when I hung up the phone, I heard God's voice so clearly. He said, "Either you're going to let this marriage die, or your ministry will die." I almost dropped my phone. It was scary, but also, I knew it was serious. I said to myself, "There is no way I'm not going to go through with this."

I told him that I was going through with it and that I was not going to be able to stay with him. He became angry and then reminded me that I couldn't put him out because his name was on the lease as well. I forgot that I had allowed him to sign the paperwork. I called the leasing manager and she told me she couldn't do anything about it and he would have to agree to the terms. I was devastated and felt so bad. Once again, God had given me all that I needed to get out. I prayed and cried every day. He became more and more disrespectful to me because he knew there was nothing I could do. He would continue to sit in my face and converse with females. He began to deal with the young lady again and left and would stay gone for days. I wanted out. There was no way I could deal with this in my home for another year. God always answers my prayers. One day the manager of the townhomes put a letter on my door saying that my husband was not added to the lease. He never turned in his verification of employment to her. She couldn't wait any longer to process the updates. I cried and cried. I was miserable and so sad about the situation. This was a blessing that I couldn't be more grateful for. God gave me a second chance to get it right. I felt a freedom and a confidence in God like never before. He was truly with me and although I didn't always listen, He showed up for me.

My husband eventually left and moved out. I began to prepare myself for our court date. Everything seemed to be lining up the way that I had desired. I was ready. I was scared but happy at the same time. I wanted to experience freedom and joy for once. I didn't care about the idea of being alone. The day finally came and I was at peace. I got up and had my coffee and prayer time. I didn't know what to expect. I knew that he was not going to show up in court. I wasn't sure if they would continue the court date because he needed to be there to finalize. I arrived at court and began to panic but in a silent way. Thankfully my big sister was with me to support me. My husband texted me as I sat there waiting for my name to be called. He said, "Please don't leave me." At that point, there was no looking back. I went through with the divorce and walked out feeling freedom. I felt a big relief. I continued to live my life in a normal way and I was ok for a while until I started noticing my children seemed to be sad a lot. Their father had nothing to do with them after our divorce. He had gone on and started a new life.

Months had gone by and there was no communication. I started to rethink my decision. Was I selfish? Did I think about the impact it would have on my children? Did I really hear God? Was it worth it? My kids were suffering and it was hard to watch as a mother. I became depressed. I felt like something had died. I never realized the aftermath of how things would be. I had been in a relationship with this man since middle school. Now I am a grown adult and he is no longer here. Although the relationship was toxic, I was still used to it. I never knew anything differently. So yes, while it was a good thing that I let it go, there was still lots of residue there. I wanted to begin to live life again but had no idea how to do that. I have never known any other man and how to even love myself. I would always keep myself busy in order to live through the pain, but then there was a void and I had no idea about what to do. I was in a darker place than before the divorce.

One day I was just sitting in my room crying; talking to God. I never allow my children to see me crying so I would always go into a secret place. I had a sign on my door so that they would know not to interrupt me. My son came to the door. He opened and closed the door a few times. He just stood there and stared at me. I became agitated because he was interrupting the time I needed alone. I yelled at him and said, "What do you want?" He opened the door, looked me in my face, and said, "I'm just trying to tell you that I miss my daddy." I couldn't even hold back the tears. I grabbed him and immediately started praying. I told him I knew it was hard and that he felt sad but we just needed to pray and ask God to help his dad get his act together so that he could become a father to them. I was crushed. It was a huge sting. That crippled me for days. I am failing my children is all that I could think about. How can I make this mess right? I was always a super mom, but this one is out of my control. It's one thing for me to hurt but to see my son, my firstborn who never really expressed his feelings, broke down nearly killed me. I would do whatever to fix any problems that my children had.

I'M BRAVE ENOUGH TO LET GO.

9

MY EXODUS

The holiday time came around and I took the children to see their father on Christmas day. They had a smile on their face I had never seen. No matter what he does to them, they love him like he's perfect. That little moment of comfort for them gave me the joy and strength that I needed. We began to converse more on the phone after that day. He called the children one day and asked if he could come over. My children came and asked me with so much excitement in their voices. I didn't want to disappoint them and say no because they hadn't been able to see him in months. I agreed and allowed him to come over. Honestly, a part of me was missing him too. I prayed and believed that he was going to get himself together and one day we would be remarried. He came over and everything was good. We ended up talking and sleeping together. I tried justifying things in my head. Well, if God is going to put us back together then nothing is wrong with this. The paper means nothing. That was me trying to justify my wrongs because I know in the eyes of God the paper does matter. The Bible says, *"Marriage is honourable in all, and the bed undefiled: but whoremongers and adulterers God will judge."* (Hebrews 13:4)

It felt good for a moment. He would stay at my house a lot. He would watch the children so that I could pick up more hours at work. We would do things as a family every day. I felt comfortable again. I didn't care what was going on outside of the house, I was just happy to see my children happy. I believed that this could turn and work in my favor; that God had dealt with him and he was able to see that life without us was not good or peaceful for him. He was consistent with his word and being there. I had no problems. But, of course, I was wrong again. Eventually, the young lady popped up.

I had sex with him one night and I can't even describe the feeling that I felt. I pushed him off of me because my spirit could not get with it. I knew this was wrong and not pleasing to God. This was on Valentine's Day in 2018. The young lady was calling his phone non-stop while he was sleeping. The next morning, I went to work and we discussed taking the kids to a kid-friendly place when I got off. He texted me while I was working and said that he was going back to his home to get more clothes and coming back. I didn't think too much of it and was ok. I got off of work and he was not back. I tried calling him and texting multiple times, but no response. I took my children out and had a good evening with them. I was mad at myself because I knew that I had allowed him to come in and lie to me again.

That night around 3:30 am, I received a phone call from an unknown caller. It was the young lady he was dealing with. She told me that she had read all of our messages, that he wasn't going to leave her alone, and that he was lying to me about everything. She told me that I was stupid for believing that she was going anywhere. There was a lot of verbal abuse and disrespect on her end. I asked her where he was. She told me that she had just had sex with him and put him to sleep. I was disgusted. I hung up the phone and just began to cry. Life just began to get crazier and crazier for me. He called me the next day and said that she had taken his phone without his permission and that he wasn't with her. Of course, I'm no fool and knew that it was a lie, but whatever. The next couple of weeks he was still coming around but there was no intimacy between us. I was only allowing him to help with the children so that I could work.

One day as I was praying, I just felt like God was going to allow me to be free and clean. The soul tie would be broken in some kind of way. He was at my home and I was preparing for a Friday night church service with my sisters. He asked me if I could drop him off at his mom's until I was finished. I agreed but let him know that I would be coming straight to pick him up so that he could watch the children the next morning while I worked. That was the night that utterly changed my life. It changed and broke a lot of things immediately. While sitting in the service worshiping and praising God, the speaker called me to the front. She stated that God kept showing her my face and that He wanted to break some things off of me. She prayed for me and I fell to the ground screaming in tears. I felt something fall off of me in a way I had never experienced before. I knew that was exactly what I needed to truly be free. I couldn't articulate on my own why I felt the need to put up with him because I was lonely or afraid. God was with me the entire time. I got up and felt so joyful. I said to myself, "It's time to let go and trust God in the way that it should be done." I left knowing that God was doing something new for me.

I arrived at his mom's house to pick him back up and he was nowhere to be found. That was the first time I had ever been able to laugh and not cry. I called him about three times and he didn't answer. I knew then that it was a wrap. I was so free from him in a way that I never knew existed. Now I could lock in and focus on my children. I felt relief from the sense of being emotionally attached to him. I felt freedom but I knew that I needed to keep a pure heart about my children. He stopped being supportive in any way because I made the decision that the relationship was dead and was never coming back to life. I desired to get along for the children's sake but no other line would be crossed. He couldn't handle that. He was having his cake and eating it even after the divorce. He would even brag about me divorcing him but still dealing with him in a way as if we were still legally married. I realized that I was doing more than settling. I had conditioned myself to believe that I was a nobody. I masked my identity in my children and stayed busy. I didn't love myself and it had nothing to do with me. It had nothing to do with my true belief about me. It was rooted in the things I dealt with as a child and then marrying someone who fed those emotions.

I started to go into a deeper depression because now I'm all the way alone. I don't have any relief from the children and the bills won't stop. My children were hurting and longing for their father and I had completely cut him off. I always left the door open for him to be a father but he became bitter. I would reach out to him about how the children were feeling and would tell him that he needed to be there for them. I reminded him of how he felt as a little boy with no father. He would read every message but not reply. I became very overwhelmed. I couldn't keep up with my bills any longer. I was barely making ends meet. The kids would want to do things and I would constantly have to tell them no. Now and again I would earn extra money or someone would bless me and I would treat the kids out to food. I wouldn't eat because there wasn't enough for me to afford a meal for myself. I didn't complain, I was just excited that I could do something special for them. Let me make this clear though, I come from a great support system and God knows had it not been for family and friends, I would not have made it through. I would never ask them for anything but they knew there was a need. I am a woman who will always try and figure things out on her own without being a burden. I just had the mindset that these are my children. It's no one's responsibility but me and their dad to make sure they are taken care of. In a way, I look back and say that was a form of pride on my end. God blessed me with loving caring people for a reason. There is no reason to be ashamed to ask for help.

I prayed and asked God to help me financially and for more

strength. It seemed like the bills were continuing to pile up to the point that I couldn't see my way out of the hole. My children became depressed in a way that I had never imagined. My oldest two began to act out in school. They became angry and disobedient to the teachers. I was stressed beyond measure. Hope just wasn't there anymore. I decided one day that this life is crap. I thought to myself, I have ruined my family's life. My children will never forgive me for bringing them into my world that was unstable and full of hell. I sat in my room one day crying uncontrollably. I had decided that it was going to be my last day on this earth. I had a bottle of pain pills that were prescribed and were ten times stronger than the normal over-the-counter ones. I didn't care about anything anymore. This world would be a better place without me and I knew this. As I began to open the top of the bottle my daughter knocked on my door and then walked into the room. She asked me if I was ok and I told her yes. I was just here praising God. I was shaking. I knew it was God once again saving my life. He sent my daughter to remind me that there is something worth fighting for. When my strength is gone, His is more than enough to sustain me. Life had seemed so hard and hopeless but at that moment I knew I had something greater to live for. I asked God for forgiveness and asked Him to please show me the way He desires for me to go. I needed to know the next steps for my life and a plan to correct all of the wrongs.

"AND YE SHALL KNOW THE TRUTH, AND THE TRUTH SHALL MAKE YOU FREE."

JOHN 8:32

10

TRUTH SPEAKS FOR ITSELF

Life started to get better. Not because of anything big or financial but because I felt alive in a way that I had never known. I knew it was very important that I fix the messes I had made with the help of God. I started by first getting my children into counseling. They would not open up to me very much but I knew it was needed. They went once a week to counseling but it didn't do much. They wouldn't talk there either. I tried to make them more comfortable with talking to me and let them know that it was ok to be hurt. They would always say that nothing was wrong and they were fine. I just continued to pray for them and asked God to heal their hearts and minds. I didn't want my children to feel like they had done something wrong and were the reason their dad wasn't around.

I was always being attacked though. He started to pop up either on the phone or in person to speak with my children. He would ask me personal questions about me dating or if I had someone around his children. I would never allow him to question me because it took the focus off of what mattered. I just couldn't understand how he could go months without seeing his children, then when he is presented with one, focuses on me. That caused more hell because he began to make statements to my children. He would tell them he wasn't their dad and they would have a new daddy when I was married again. It was sickening to listen to. I tried and tried to keep quiet because I didn't want to ruin my children's happy moments. It became old though. Eventually, I had to speak up and let him know that it wasn't cool. He became irate and left and told the children he was gone and never coming back. He told them it was my fault when clearly I was the one striving to keep the peace.

It took a long while for me to allow him to come back to my home or even communicate with the children. It was like a huge emotional setback. I bit my tongue all the time in front of the children because I also understood that they would get older and see him for exactly who he was. It was always hard to continue to choose to be the bigger person but I did it. Even with some of his family members, he caused a lot of tension with his lies and accusations about me. They judged me based on the things he said to them. But once we were divorced and he had to live with them, they saw him more often than normal. They would tell me how they saw exactly what I meant and that he was the problem. The problem always takes care of itself.

One day he came to my home and was playing around with the kids. He was playing with my oldest daughter a little too rough and she became upset. He cursed her out and called her the B-word. I was furious. She began to cry like I've never seen before. That was the first time my children saw me that upset with him and I didn't care. He was threatening to hit me and I had to pull a knife and kick him out. I blacked out. I didn't care at that moment what was happening. How dare you disrespect my child in that manner in front of my face. On top of me already stressing, having to allow him in my home when he was giving me no support was hard. He left out of the home and would not stop beating on my door. I allowed him back in because he said that he wanted to apologize to her. He did and at that moment she was not in a space of receiving. He got angry all over again and said that he meant it and she was dead to him. He never wanted her to speak to him again is what he said. I was in shock. How did this even happen? Of course, he was intoxicated from the beginning. I told my children right then and there that he could never step foot in my home. My son was crushed. He was taking his dad's side and told my daughter that she was doing too much; that she took things too far because their dad was just playing. There was tension in our home for a while. I felt like a failure. My kids will never be the same. They are traumatized at such a young age. There was absolutely nothing I could do about it besides trust the One who created them. God was my only hope.

Months went by and it seemed as if their dad had disappeared from the face of the earth. One day I was just talking with my son and asked if he had heard from his dad. He said, "No, not since the day he came over last," which was the day that he cursed my daughter out. I asked what form of communication was there. He told me he texted him after and began to show me the text. As I was reading, I had to hold back the tears. As I'm writing this now, I'm doing the same. My son had texted his father that he was sorry that things happened to him the way they did and that he loved him. He was taking the blame for his dad just to be able to have a relationship with him. It was so heartbreaking as a mother to see that. It broke my heart even more that his dad never replied. I am shedding tears as I write. It's bringing back so many emotions.

My son is now 18 years old and I am sure he still struggles with his father not being around as often as he should, but for a kid to take the blame just to have his father reminds me of myself. I would rather take the blame and deal with anything than be alone. I am glad that I broke that cycle before it was way too late. Every relationship with your parents is really important, but I believe the father and son relationship is sooo important, especially with the days and times we are living in, and for my son to be a statistic without having his father around is the worst feeling. I would give anything to see him have a healthy relationship with his father. The relationship between them now is there and with the girls, but it's not on a normal basis. My children love their father so much and they pray daily for him. He is around sporadically but they are older now and understand the way things are. In their eyes, he can do no wrong.

I'M FINALLY LEARNING TO LOVE MYSELF.

11

THE PERFECT MISFIT

Life is really what you make it. I made a decision that I could no longer allow life to beat me down. I'm going to fight in a way that I have never fought before. I looked into filing bankruptcy because I had so much debt and saw no other way. I had purchased a vehicle and was lucky enough that the car lot allowed me to pay the amount of my down payment in increments. I was paying a car note for about a year before the engine went out. The car lot refused to do anything because they stated the warranty had already expired. The repair was going to cost more than $6,000. I barely had $6 in my account. My credit was horrible and I needed a vehicle badly. I also had a voluntary repossession before this vehicle because I couldn't keep up with payments. I had taken out loans from companies online and in my state. The interest rates were ridiculous. I was paying triple the amount that I borrowed.

One day I was at work and forgot that it was payday for me because I hadn't gotten a notification of a deposit from the bank. I just so happened to check my account and the check was much less than what it should have been. I went to HR to find out what was going on. They informed me that my checks were being garnished due to medical bills. I didn't recall having anything on my record. The only surgery I had was for my broken jaw, but my insurance had covered that. I quickly learned that my checks were being garnished from my ex-husband's medical bills. I had signed off on the care for him when he got shot, not even realizing I was making myself responsible for his debt. I knew nothing about this. They had been sending him info about court dates and everything but he never responded. Of course, he hid his income so they weren't able to take the money from him. They told me that I needed to find out where he was working so that they could get the money from him or that I would have to keep paying.

Enough was enough. I filed for bankruptcy and had a clean slate. Now life was looking up for me. I was able to at least keep the bills paid and have some extra left over. I began to date myself for a while. I wanted to learn what I liked and to love myself for once. I started to accept a lot of things were permanently different. I was no longer trying to fix another person or mask my pain with work and being a mom. I took a few trips alone, and I must say, it was one of the best decisions I had ever made. It was really weird in the beginning because it was definitely out of my comfort zone, but it was worth it. I felt like I could do this solo thing and it allowed me to explore life. I hadn't done much outside of work and taking care of my children and my family. Oh man did I discover that I had been missing out big time.

It seemed like I was meeting a lot of women who were going through or had already gone through a divorce. Our stories were similar. Most of the women were much older than I was but I found myself being able to help them in major ways. They would call me often to talk and when they just needed some support. We would cry, pray, and laugh together often. I started to realize more and more that the pain and hurt that I experienced were for a much greater purpose than I ever even imagined. I began to ask God to show me my identity in Him, and more importantly, His purpose for my life regarding other women.

Fashion and weird clothes were always my thing. I felt like I never belonged with normal people. Not in a bad way, but I was truly set apart. I wasn't able to dress up much and feel pretty during the time I was struggling in the marriage. So, when I decided to start dating myself, I slowly began to feel better. One day as I was getting dressed, I immediately just felt a shift in my spirit, and I looked in the mirror once I was fully finished and saw a beautiful masterpiece. I just felt absolutely fabulous. That's when God plainly began to speak to me. Although clothing doesn't fix internal pain, it helped me on this journey. And let's be honest whether male or female, we all feel better with our hair done and wearing nice clothing. It brings a different level of confidence.

I wanted to have a women's clothing store one day. I have dreamed of attending Fashion Week in Paris since I can remember as a child. God had dropped the name Misfits Clothing Boutique inside of me. I felt a big fire inside of my body. God was letting me know at that moment that it was ok to be different. I was definitely without a doubt a MISFIT, but society looks at that word as something negative and a person that you would want to stay far away from, and that is what causes a lot of misfits to bend and stay small. They can't be themselves because they are so worried about the opinions of others. To me, it meant although I was not normal and different, it was a great thing. A misfit to me means that all while being yourself; wearing whatever you want; standing out, and using clothing as a way to express yourself, you belong but you don't belong at the same time. I was being set up the entire time and had no idea. All of the times I felt that I needed to compromise who I was to satisfy others was a lie. Satan wanted me to hate being myself because he knew that God was calling me to be different for His glory. Many women and men would feel like they had to fit in. They would compromise who they are for others just for a sense of belonging. No more. I was ready. I understood the assignment and now I can play the game the right way. It clicked that we sometimes feel like we are sloppy, out of shape, and just worthless, but once we decide to get up, get dressed, and enjoy this beautiful thing called life, we feel supernatural strength.

"FOR GOD HATH NOT GIVEN US THE SPIRIT OF FEAR; BUT OF POWER, AND OF LOVE, AND OF A SOUND MIND."

2 TIMOTHY 1:7

12

FEAR IS NOT MY FUTURE

I prayed and prayed and decided to go ahead and start the process of starting my store. I knew that I wanted to start online so I did my research on how to get things going. In March of 2019, I announced via social media that I was starting my store. I was nervous as heck because I had no idea what I was doing. Honestly, I was just doing something to try and see what feedback I was going to receive. It turned out much better than I could have even imagined. It was tough and still is because I didn't have many resources for help, but God has placed so many people in my life who have helped me in so many ways, unselfishly, and I am more than grateful for that.

People were so complimentary of the name. They found it to be unique but also fitting for me. I would release inventory and they would always say they love my style. They would tell me how they have always loved the way that I dressed and thought that I was unique. They told me how beautiful they thought I was and a kind person. I am far from some of the images that were portrayed, but they gave me hope again. I began to come alive in a way that I had longed for. Of course, I had many people come in and try to discourage me. They would say, "Girl it's a million boutiques. Why would you try and start one now?" I also had someone who was an associate from one of the churches I visited who bought a shirt with the Misfits logo on there. After she had posted herself in the shirt on social media, she texted me and said that someone told her that Misfits was associated with negativity and had a bad reputation. I won't even lie, for a moment I felt discouraged. The thing is, I never desired to do anything to compromise myself or my relationship with God. With her saying that to me, and I can almost bet that it was someone in the church, I felt like I made a mistake. The enemy began to attack my mind about this. I had tons of people celebrating and then this one comment from this person came and crippled me. I started to think about conversations that were possibly being had about me with certain individuals. Nevertheless, I didn't let it bother me for too long. Thankfully I had enough of the right people, my family and friends encouraging me to keep going.

Being in business for yourself is no joke. I did all I could and took advantage of the free tools that were available to me. In the midst of this, I decided that I was going to take advantage of this momentum. I am a lover of food. Always have been. I always tell everyone that I am not a materialistic girl. I love to eat well and travel. My next husband is going to love me for that. He will never have to worry about me spending all of our money on piling up clothes and things that really won't hold much value. Anyway, I digressed. I would oftentimes post myself eating or traveling to new restaurants on social media. Many people would comment on the post and say, "Girl you need to take me with you. You are always eating well and know all of the good restaurants." I was getting that feedback so much that I decided to take them up on that offer.

I started a Misfits foodie group. I wanted to combine my love for fashion and thrifting with my love for food. I decided that once a month I would invite a group of ladies out. We would go to the thrift store, and then have lunch. This group was open to anyone as long as the respect was kept. The first meetup was a great success. I mean, I wasn't expecting many people to show up because it was pretty much strangers joining in one setting, but I stepped out on faith. The feedback was great and everyone was excited and could hardly wait for me to do it again. They even gave suggestions about maybe doing an annual trip together. I was in awe. Once again God was proving to me that I was the proof. Everything that was sent to break me was helping to build me. Now don't get me wrong, I was still constantly struggling in all areas, but I was determined not to let my circumstances get the best of me. I knew that I didn't have to worry because the fight was already fixed.

I gained some great relationships with many different people; women and men. It became easier to share my story and to be transparent. It was like a breath of fresh air to many because they didn't feel that being transparent was a good thing to do. They were afraid of being judged. People began to ask me to speak to an audience telling my story. I would become nervous right beforehand. When I would speak, I would think to myself the entire time, I am doing a horrible job. I would even begin to stumble in my words. At one particular event that I was a part of - which is a mentoring group I'm a part of - my mentor asked me to be one of the speakers. She said that God had given her instructions to have me speak and share just five minutes of my testimony. Now this was an annual event so I knew that there was going to be a large crowd there. Of course, I wasn't going to say no, although I wanted to. I had prepared words to speak over and over on notebook paper. I went over them in the mirror a few times. I wanted to be sure that I told the story in a way that wouldn't leave out hope. Yes, my experiences were not the greatest, but something special came from them.

The day came when I was supposed to speak. I took my notebook with me to the event because I decided that I would just read word for word. I knew the time was good because as I was rehearsing it at home it was a little under four minutes. The event had a few curve balls and it took much longer than anticipated to start. This caused slight shifts in the speaker's time. I had in the back of my mind that I had to condense my speech. I couldn't figure out how to cut it down. I had studied for weeks to make sure I was not going to embarrass myself. My friend was there with me and I asked her if she had any ideas on what I should say. She wrote some things down for me that made sense but something said, "No." I heard the voice of God once again. He said, "Regina, you don't need any of that. I am with you. I have gone before you. Go forth and just open your mouth and I will give you exactly what to say." I knew then I was going to do just fine. Although the nervousness was there, nothing was going to be able to hold me back, because God was resting in me and reassuring me that I would be ok.

The time finally came when they called all of the speakers to come to the stage. Whew, seems like it took forever and my nerves were jumping. There were about 12 ladies who were speaking. As soon as we got on the stage, our mentor whispered to us and said, "We have to cut the time down from five minutes to now three minutes. I was already prepared for that, but of course, that caused my mind to become restless. I was about the seventh or eighth person to speak. All of the women did so well. I started to compare myself to them and doubt. They spoke so eloquently. They knew the Word and could articulate it so well into their story. I felt like Moses. I quickly said a prayer and told God, "I trust You." I said, "This is not about me, but You. Whatever I say, please let it reach a few people." I began to speak and all of my nerves were calmed. It was like me and God were the only ones there. I spoke from a place in my heart. While I was speaking, people were screaming at me saying, "C'mon girl." I heard my mentor on the side of me saying, "Come on Regina." It was an experience I'll never forget.

Once I was finished people all over the room stood to their feet applauding and screaming, "Great job." I was so blessed in my spirit. The host was a male. He stood, wrapped his arm around my shoulder, and said, "Look around this room." He said, "This is just a glimpse of what God is going to do in your life." He said God was showing me where He was taking me and that I would be helping many women across the nations. I could finally breathe. I had many people coming to me after that event, and even to this day, saying how much they were blessed by my testimony. God is amazing.

I
DESERVE
PEACE.

13

OLD WAYS WON'T OPEN NEW DOORS

Some great things have taken place in my life. I got out of my comfort zone and quickly found out that I am really a social butterfly and in the same way that I love people, they do love me back. Fear of failure and lost hope can have you in a place of wanting to give up on everything. I always look back and say, "What if God had allowed me to take my life?" That was very selfish of me to even allow those thoughts to take over my mind. At the same time that I started my boutique and foodie group, I was introduced to another opportunity to make more income. I was still working as a home health aide for a large company here in Missouri. I loved the clients so much and they all fell in love with me. We became like family. The work was great as well. It wasn't as heavy of a workload as the nursing home, which is the reason I initially transitioned. The pay was the problem.

Although I had been given a fresh start on my finances by filing bankruptcy it still just wasn't enough. I oftentimes hear people saying how you should be able to afford certain things because you make a certain amount of money on a job. What they don't realize is that the taxes being taken out eat away at the portion you have for yourself. I will never look down on anyone who is struggling or because of the amount of money they make. You cannot judge a book by its cover. I am a very hard worker and I went above and beyond my duties with no extra pay. I never complained but the hours worked and the money I was being paid just didn't add up. Plus, I wanted to be home more with my children. I didn't want them to have to grow up too fast because I was working and needed their help like an adult while still being teenagers.

One of my former co-workers reached out to me about assisting her with some training hours for a new opportunity she was entering into. Now being the person that I am, I didn't ask a lot of questions. If my girls called for anything, as long as it was legal and didn't require me to fight, I was going to be there. This is when I was introduced to an opportunity that changed my life and mindset. The unbelievable part is that I was introduced to this same opportunity while I was married. I knew at the time that it wouldn't work because of the hell my husband would give me. On top of that, it was not your normal nine to five and the head coach was a man. So, I knew that working closely with him would cause chaos. The opportunity was for me to become a licensed life insurance agent. I never thought much about life insurance but I knew that I needed it.

While in nursing school, one of my instructors, who is also a part of the company, educated me about it. I got a policy with her for my family and she also presented me with the opportunity to make extra income. I asked God was this a sign for me to go ahead and get involved with this. Plus, I needed to make the extra income and it was legal. I didn't hesitate for long. I decided to give this thing a try. I would still be doing what I loved, which is helping people, just in a different way. I knew that life insurance was important, especially after almost losing my husband when he was shot. I went in head first. I needed something new and this surely expanded my thought process a lot. I was always the woman who never wanted to live in poverty forever. While I appreciate every government assistance program that I qualified for, I wanted to use that as a stepping stone to one day become financially free.

I attended one event before I officially signed my paperwork to join the company. It was mind-blowing. To see so many people have success from helping our community was amazing. Not only were these people making hundreds of thousands of dollars per year, some even made millions. A lot of them were African Americans. They had similar backgrounds as myself. They came from nothing and this opportunity changed their life. I didn't know everything at the time but I was willing to learn. The more I learned, the more I went and told others. I was skeptical at first because I heard things about the company that weren't good. A lot of people were saying it was a scam and that you wouldn't make money here, but that was nowhere near my story. On top of that, I had already purchased the insurance coverage before I joined the business as an agent.

So, once I got into the business and began to meet people who could help me have success, I decided I would put the time in to learn as much as I could. I never knew that the business was so lucrative. I began to make good money without working as many hours as my nine-to-five. I prayed and felt like God was leading me to focus on that for a while and stop the home health care job. It only made sense when I considered the time and the money I made on the job. I would also be able to create my own schedule which meant more flexibility and time with my children. My coach also had many conversations with me about giving the opportunity a real shot and not being afraid to soar. He told me to give my job just a 30-day notice that I was taking a leave of absence. He wanted me to just take a chance on myself and see if the business would work well enough for me to leave my job. I worked my butt off for the next 30 days as if my life depended on it. I understood that I was giving up the security of having a sure income for a commission-based job. I must say that I was not disappointed at all. I made $7,000 within those 30 days that I took off from my job. That was more money than I could even think about making in a month. I was only bringing in somewhere between $1,200 and $1,700 per month from work. It was a no-brainer for me at that point. I knew that was my sign to leave and take a chance on myself and my business.

This opportunity also opened up other doors for me to network and travel all around. The trips were always a good time and I learned so much from many different people who were willing to share their wisdom and knowledge with me. I will forever be grateful. I was able to use the money that I had earned from selling the life insurance policies to not only pay my bills but also to fund Misfits. I was able to do many things for my children for a while that normally would take months for me to save to do. They could ask me for anything and I would get it with no hesitation. This is also another reason why I decided that I was going to work hard to be a better woman, mom, friend, and business owner. I wanted to have success for many different reasons, but being able to do things for my children was one that was at the top of the list. I have the most grateful children I've ever met. I am currently still a licensed life insurance agent and I enjoy every moment of it. Teaching others about the importance of insurance and being able to save and invest is a joy I can't explain. The kids even send me referrals now. It's the funniest thing ever.

I
WILL
NOT DOUBT
MY VALUE
AND
MY POWER
EVER
AGAIN.

14

STRENGTH LIKE NO OTHER

The past few years of life have been rough. Although great things have happened, I battle in my mind daily about different things. I am tormented a lot in my mind and I know that hinders my growth so much. I recently started going to therapy again and it has caused many emotions to rise up in me. I never really got deep into conversations about my past in a way that forced me to dig deep to figure out the parts of me that are not fully healed. I get so emotional because I never looked at life in the way that I do now. Literally every experience that we have is not so pleasant. If it's not corrected in the right way, it can follow us into adulthood and do significant damage if we are not careful. I am just really glad that I have the mindset to want to learn and grow into the true woman that I am destined to be.

I have been thrown many curve balls. The business is up and down. I am constantly trying to find ways to make it work. Gratefully, I was able to finally hire some help to grow my business. God is so amazing and such a provider. I was always afraid to invest in myself, but in all honesty, I couldn't afford to. But I had to step out on faith and just do it. The way will be made. I have taken breaks from the boutique many times and felt like giving up because it seemed that I was never going to figure things out. I also felt that I was never going to be able to compete or compare with the stores that were already around.

The enemy is the father of lies. He will do whatever to keep you from fulfilling God's plan for your life. I know now that every time he attacks me in a certain way, he wants to discourage me from doing the work that God has called me to do. Not only that, but I have had many run-ins with my children. They went through a season where it seemed like they were being rebellious a lot. I just didn't understand what was going on. They would question everything I told them to do and still decide not to listen to me. I kept holding on to them in a way that I see now as control. My job isn't to argue with them. So, I did all I could. I began to just pray for each of them and ask God to first give me strength and then also for him to heal their hearts. I prayed for their protection and their minds so that they wouldn't fall into a hard place. I understand that being a kid nowadays is hard, but you have to trust your children. They eventually came around and now they are the joys of my heart. I love them to pieces. I couldn't be more proud of my oldest two. They have stepped up in many ways to help me with their younger sibling and with keeping the house in order.

I have encountered many children who experienced broken homes. They have been traumatized from watching their parents be abused. I have a true heart to help so many people in many different ways. I have been building my life based on what I know God is calling me to do. The last few years have been rough, but I have been surviving the best way I can. I am still working through dealing with my emotions and learning more self-control. It is very difficult having children with a man who refuses to take care of his responsibility. I say that because he is still around although he's not there on a normal basis. I had to ask God to help my heart and mood when dealing with him. When I was initially released from him at the church service, emotionally I had no feelings for him. In fact, to this day, unless a thought comes to mind or someone mentions his name, I sort of forget that he exists. But I am wise enough to know that I can't be selfish because of my children. If I had my way, I would prefer that he didn't come around or contact my children at all. In my opinion, more damage is done when you are in and out instead of just deciding to be fully in or fully out.

I still get upset at times when I think about the struggles I continue to face alone with my children. I am the sole provider for everything and it should have never been this way. Yes, we make decisions and have to suffer consequences, but at some point, you would like to believe that a person will change and do what's needed for their children. It's no joke being a single mom and I wouldn't wish this on my worst enemy. Yes, God provides, but I still have to always be willing to work harder and be ready to have curve balls thrown at me in my finances because he is not helping to provide.

My oldest two children are workers now. They work hard and I am grateful for that. They see and understand the value of a dollar and how hard you have to work to make ends meet. They try to buy everything they need and want themselves, but I always tell them they don't have to do that. I am still their mother. Their response is always, "Why would we make you buy it when we have our own money?" They know exactly how to make my heart smile. They even help to provide for my youngest child when she asks me for things that I can't give her at the moment. They have helped me to extend more grace to others in my life. They have shown much love to their father. For holidays and his birthdays, they always make sure that he receives a gift of some sort from them. They know that he doesn't provide for them and that he is always making broken promises, yet they don't allow their hearts to get cold. The level of patience and love they show helps me to be able to be in the same room with him and not be upset. I am grateful to God that he has blessed me with some tremendous children. It's amazing because we are the parents but we can learn so much about how to love, forgive, and have grace on others from the children. We all need it, and as hard as it is for me, I always pray for my ex-husband. I make sure that I am doing things to keep my spirit full.

He was incarcerated last year for a few months. Prior to this, he came to my home and was very mean and rude to me because I spoke about him allowing my underage children to drive the car he was in. The disrespect was on another level and he ended the conversation by telling me that I was dead to him. I won't lie and say that it didn't sting, because it did. Words are so powerful and hurt more than people realize. But I made a choice not to let it bother me and asked God to fight for me, which I know that He was already doing. While he was incarcerated, he called me asking if I could help him purchase some items because he needed warmer clothes and money for food and personal items. I wanted to say no, but God wouldn't allow me to. I thought to myself, honestly this man does nothing to help me with his children. He is not the father he should be in the physical aspect, and he knows how hard I am working to provide. Yet, he has the audacity to call me and ask me for money. I thought to myself, good, that's what he gets. I wish I would give him a dime. But I was convicted and I saw how easy it was for me to get a hard heart towards him.

He never even asked about how the children were doing when he called. He got straight to the point about him needing money. Even after the money was sent, he called again a few weeks later asking for more money without ever saying thank you the first time. I will say this to anyone who struggles with forgiveness, remember that it is always for you, not the other person. It is one of the hardest things in the world to forgive and help a person who has wronged you and it seems that they will never apologize or turn from their ways. Do it for yourself. Unforgiveness blocks blessings and can cause sickness. I want to be mad and bitter with him all the time. My flesh does, but I must remember the seventy times seven rule, *"Then came Peter to him, and said, Lord, how oft shall my brother sin against me, and I forgive him? till seven times? Jesus saith unto him, I say not unto thee, Until seven times: but, Until seventy times seven."* (Matthew 18:21-22)

It seems like people are getting away with murder at times, but it's all a false appearance. I know that my ex-husband struggles every day with the decisions that he has made. He drinks more to hide the pain. I am not even upset with him. If anything, I am sad that he is allowing life to beat him down. I am glad that I have the mind to continue to fight. I have made mistakes and I am still paying for them, but I refuse to give up. I have had many conversations with my ex-husband letting him know that he is forgiven. I forgive him and God does. Even after the divorce, I have even tried to help him get his life on track and be a better man. It's really all about making a decision. I can't make him want better, but I can let him know that it is available for him. I'm often told by people who may run into him that he always talks about me. He always says that I was the best thing that ever happened to him. He speaks highly of me to others and I can appreciate that. I never was the woman who talked him down to others after the divorce. Of course, I would speak about him not helping with his children and how he left a huge burden on me, but that is just a part of my testimony and me being honest, but it's never in a disrespectful way. At the end of it all, I want everyone to live in the freedom of God and know that they can be forgiven. Something that may seem impossible to turn around is very possible. As long as you have breath in your body, there is grace and mercy that is available for you. Hopefully one day he will understand this, and I will continue to pray for him and trust God for his salvation. One day he will have a testimony to share about how he was forgiven and turned his life around, and he became the best father that his children could have ever imagined. There is hope.

I

AM

NOT

THE

TRAUMA

I

EXPERIENCED.

15

THE FINISHING TOUCH

Here I am today, going through many emotions that have come back up as I am writing this book. I am more than excited about what will come from this. Life has been challenging for me this past year. With inflation and my children growing older, I have had mixed emotions. I have had to pick up more work hours and just really focus on maintaining my household. It has caused some stress but not to the point where I am ready to lose my mind. I have seen God's hand this year in my life in a way that I have never seen before. I have also continued to think about how I can help others. I have run into women and men this past year who are experiencing the same struggles I did. I knew that God was calling me to really lock in and get serious about my calling. There are many people who feel like all hope is lost. I am drawing these kinds of people into my life because they need to know that there is much more life to live. They need to know that there is freedom for them.

I want to use my gifts and calling to be a voice for people. I am not afraid to speak up and have a bold attitude. It was hard for me to be myself initially because of the fear of what others may think. I am still insecure in some ways, but freedom is a real process. I take life day by day and fight with a clear mind. I am learning that if you can get control of your mind, you will have a great life. If we allow ourselves to meditate on things that are negative, it will grow and we will start to believe lies about ourselves. I can see the day coming when my kids will be able to share their testimony about what God has done for us. They will one day open up and sincerely express how their life impacted their belief. I know that they are hurting and won't speak now, but I am praying that God will allow them to share their story with other young people who need help. We all have a calling on our lives that is much greater than us. We never understand it until we have to share it. I have learned myself. I am proud to say that I am grateful for the pruning, the teaching, the tests, and the trials. I have been able to look in the mirror and love myself again. I don't concern myself with my past. I have a bright future ahead.

Some days I am rocking out this thing called life and sometimes it's rocking me. My mind goes to so many places daily. I feel like I can conquer the world. I have so many ideas and people that I want to include. I am so happy that I am writing this book at this time. I know that God has prepared me for such a time as this.

I was sitting at home relaxing one day and thought about going on the news to share my business and the mission behind it. I also was on a fast that day. I had hired the marketing team and knew that I needed to do more things to get exposure. I went online to fill out the paperwork to have a segment on one of my local news channels, Fox 2. I was shocked because I got a call within the next hour. The host, Tim Ezell, called me and said that he was so impressed with my story and asked if I could come on the next day to do my segment. I told him that was too soon and I wasn't expecting to hear back from them so fast. I scheduled it for the following week and boy was I a nervous wreck. I prayed and asked God to help me once again to make sense and not be nervous. The segment was only about three minutes long, so I had to be prepared. This appearance was different from the speaking engagement because more people would be tuning in, and there was no chance to correct anything because the show aired live.

I had a friend come with me for support. I fasted that morning and didn't talk to anyone on the phone. I was in the studio walking back and forth and just praying silently. The time came for me to go live and I began to pray real fast (*lol*). I went live and started to speak. Every question I was asked I felt like I was screwing the interview up. I was wishing in my mind the entire time that it would hurry up and be over with. I finally finished and my friend told me that I did a great job. I thought, "Really? You're just saying anything. That was terrible," but that wasn't a lie, I guess. I gathered my things together and as I left, I checked my phone. Within minutes, I had so many messages from people who were tuned in saying so many great things. I hadn't told many people about my appearance outside of family and friends because I didn't want anyone trying to discourage me. I was in shock. Honestly, I shed a few tears afterward because I just knew that it was bad, but the feedback was amazing.

I logged onto my social media and that's when reality got crazy. Many people commented on my wall and said how proud they were of me. It showed me that I doubt myself and that there is something deeper going on for me to feel so awful. I would literally self-sabotage my own creative unique style and makeup. God made no mistakes when he gave me the name MISFITS. I am supposed to be different and unique. I am supposed to be bold and on certain platforms. My prayer every day is for God to use me for His glory and His only. I was so blown away by the TV appearance and felt like I was on cloud nine. I knew God was reminding me of His promises over my life. He was letting me know that no matter what things looked like, He was there the entire time. His plans and purposes for my life were already written, just like He promised in Jeremiah 29:11, *"For I know the thoughts that I think toward you, saith the LORD, thoughts of peace, and not of evil, to give you an expected end."* I felt a glow and butterflies that I had not felt in a very long time.

The next day, I was in my car running some errands. My car is really like my altar with God. We have some of the best conversations. I was praying and God dropped in my spirit that now was the time for me to really share my story, but not just in the way I had been doing it. He told me that it was time for me to write the book He had told me years before that I would be writing. I mean it was so clear. He told me to start writing immediately. Now I was in a place of knowing that God was truly speaking and I needed to listen and obey. I kid you not, not even five minutes later, I pulled up to Walmart to shop for groceries. I opened up my social media, Instagram to be exact, and I had a DM from Larry Rodgers, co-founder of ForWord Books publishing company. He stated that he saw my interview on the news the day before and was interested in helping me publish my story in a book. I literally threw my phone in tears of joy. I couldn't believe it.

Everything was lining up the way that I needed it to. God confirmed Himself over and over that the story was much bigger than I can even imagine. Many women are silent in their relationships and are battling feeling like they can't make it out. I want to share the story of hope and belief. I want them to know there is so much freedom in trusting God when He says He will be with you.

I want you to know that the first step to true healing is to forgive. You are beautiful. You are worthy. Your trials and tribulations all came to make you stronger. God is working all things together for your good. You are going to be just fine. Trust me, this is just a glimpse of what I have gone through. I couldn't even begin to write about the mental anguish that I have had to endure: the guilt that continues to rise up from time to time; me watching my children every day growing up faster than I would like; thinking about how their lives will be when they are grown and gone from my home; praying that they do not repeat the same vicious cycles that

I did, but trusting that through it all, God wants to do something so amazing for us all. It's ok to cry, scream, kick, whatever, but never give up. The world needs you. Your family needs you. And most importantly you need you. Don't let anyone dim your light anymore. Get up, dust yourself off, and fight the good fight of faith. Look fear in the face and tell it, "No more bondage. I am free. I am loved. I am somebody. I don't belong to you." What's coming is much better than what's been for me.

I feel so accomplished in writing this book. This is one of the biggest accomplishments I have achieved in a very long time. I am truly proud of myself. I can honestly say this is one charge that I have been given that doesn't have me nervous to release. I did get very transparent in my sharing but I feel like it was needed. It's time out for playing games and hiding behind masks. I refuse to do it any longer. They say that makeup is the finishing touch to a perfect outfit, but I say that me releasing this book is the FINISHING TOUCH for this chapter in my life. I can walk even more boldly now that the truth is out. No more condemnation, fear, or doubt. This is the beginning of something great. I can hardly wait to see what the future holds.

SURVIVOR'S EXERCISE

This portion of the book *Finishing Touch: A Survivor's Journey* is a five-part writing exercise for the survivors and eyewitnesses of domestic violence to participate in. I found out that writing is a form of healing and freedom for one's heart, mind, body, and soul. This is an opportunity for you to express your true sentiments and thoughts. Everyone has a story, whether good or bad, and this show of confidence, by sharing your story like I did mine, will definitely change someone's life for the better. So write the vision and make it plain. Don't allow fear and doubt, the evil twins of life, to hinder or stop you from being bold and brave in telling your story. Likewise, in spite of the abuse you may have suffered, I encourage you not to allow hatred, bitterness, and unforgiveness for the person who abused you to dictate you writing your story in a malicious manner. Speak the truth with positivity, love, and strength. The Bible says, *"And they overcame him by the blood of the Lamb, and by the word of their testimony..."* Revelation 12:11

EXERCISE ONE:

I WILL BE COURAGEOUS ENOUGH TO LEAVE AND SEEK HELP, AND
HERE'S WHY...

FINISHING TOUCH

EXERCISE TWO:

I MADE UP IN MY MIND FROM THIS DAY FORWARD THAT I AM BEAUTIFUL AND DESERVE REAL LOVE, AND HERE'S WHY...

_____

_____

_____

_____

_____

_____

_____

_____

_____

_____

_____

_____

_____

_____

_____

_____

_____

_____

EXERCISE THREE:

I WILL NO LONGER BE IN DENIAL. IT'S NOT MY FAULT, AND HERE'S WHY...

_____

_____

_____

_____

_____

_____

_____

_____

_____

_____

_____

_____

_____

_____

_____

_____

_____

_____

_____

_____

_____

_____

_____

_____

_____

_____

_____

_____

_____

_____

_____

_____

_____

_____

_____

_____

_____

_____

_____

_____

_____

_____

EXERCISE FOUR:

I AM WORTH IT, AND HERE'S WHY...

_____

_____

_____

_____

_____

_____

_____

_____

_____

_____

_____

_____

_____

_____

_____

_____

_____

_____

EXERCISE FIVE:

I DESERVE GOD'S VERY BEST IN A RELATIONSHIP, AND HERE'S WHY...

_____

_____

_____

_____

_____

_____

_____

_____

_____

_____

_____

_____

_____

_____

_____

_____

_____

_____

_____

FINISHING TOUCH

FINISHING TOUCH

_____

_____

_____

_____

_____

_____

_____

_____

_____

_____

_____

_____

_____

_____

_____

_____

_____

_____

_____

_____

_____

_____

TEEN DOMESTIC VIOLENCE STATISTICS

Statistics show that 1 in 3 U.S. teens will experience physical, sexual, or emotional abuse from someone they're in a relationship with before they become adults.

Nearly half (43%)of U.S. college women report experiencing violence or abuse while dating.

Teen dating domestic violence can take place online, or through technology. It is a type of intimate partner violence (IPV) that includes four forms of violence that can occur within the dating relationships of adolescents and young adults:

FORM 1

Physical violence: the intentional use of physical force, which includes hitting, pushing, shoving, grabbing, restraining, or using strength against someone

FORM 2

Sexual violence: forcing someone to take part in a sexual act (e.g., kissing, touching, sexual intercourse) or a non-physical sexual event (e.g., sexting) when the person does not or cannot consent

FORM 3

Psychological aggression: the use of verbal and non-verbal communication with the intent to cause mental or emotional harm, or exert control over someone

FORM 4

Stalking: a pattern of repeated, unwanted attention and contact that causes fear or concern for one's own safety or the safety of someone else (e.g., family member, close friend)

When any form of dating violence is perpetrated using technology, such as text messaging, or direct messaging (also known as DM's) and social media, it is referred to as digital dating abuse. Examples include sending sexual pictures of a dating partner to others without consent, sending or posting insulting or threatening messages, and sharing negative rumors about the person. This type of abuse has led to many individuals committing suicide due to the ridicule and pressure of being exposed to the public.

If you or someone you know is or has experienced this type of behavior, contact the National Domestic Violence Hotline at 1.800.799-SAFE (7233), text "Start" to 88788 or chat live at thehotline.org.

ADULT DOMESTIC VIOLENCE STATISTICS

Statistics report that approximately 20 people per minute will be physically abused by an intimate partner in the United States of America. In one year, this equates to more than 10 million women as well as men.

1 in 4 women and 1 in 9 men have experienced severe physical violence, sexual violence, and/or stalking by intimate partners with impacts such as injury, fearfulness, post-traumatic stress disorder, use of victim services, contraction of sexually transmitted diseases, and a plethora of other issues.

- **1 in 3 women and 1 in 4 men** have experienced some form of physical violence by an intimate partner. This includes a range of behaviors (e.g. slapping, shoving, pushing) and in some cases might not be considered "domestic violence."
- **1 in 7 women and 1 in 25 men** have been injured by an intimate partner.
- **1 in 10 women** have been raped by an intimate partner. Data is unavailable on male victims.

1 in 4 women and 1 in 7 men have been victims of severe physical violence (e.g. beating, burning, strangling) by an intimate partner in their lifetime.

1 in 7 women and 1 in 18 men have been stalked by an intimate partner during their lifetime to the point in which they felt very fearful or believed that they or someone close to them would be harmed or killed.

On a typical day, there are more than 20,000 phone calls placed to domestic violence hotlines nationwide.

The presence of a gun in a domestic violence situation increases the risk of homicide by 500%.

Intimate partner violence accounts for 15% of all violent crime.

Women between the ages of 18-24 are most commonly abused by an intimate partner.

19% of domestic violence involves a weapon.

Domestic victimization is correlated with a higher rate of depression and suicidal behavior.

Only 34% of people who are injured by intimate partners receive medical care for their injuries.

Sexual Assault

1 in 5 women and 1 in 71 men in the United States are victims of rape or attempted rape during their lifetime.

Almost half of female (46.7%) and male (44.9%) victims of rape in the United States were raped by an acquaintance. Of these, 45.4% of female rape victims and 29% of male rape victims were raped by an intimate partner.

From 2016 through 2018 the number of rape/sexual assault victimizations in the United States increased by 146%.

Stalking

Stalking victimization involves a pattern of harassing or threatening tactics used by a perpetrator that causes the victim to fear for their safety or the safety of others.

19.3 million women and 5.1 million men in the United States have been stalked in their lifetime.

60.8% of female stalking victims and 43.5% of men reported being stalked by a current or former intimate partner.

1 in 10 women and 1 in 50 men have experienced stalking by an intimate partner during their lifetime.

Homicide

A study of intimate partner homicides found that 20% of victims were not the intimate partners themselves, but family members, friends, neighbors, persons who intervened, law enforcement responders, or bystanders.

1 in 2 female murder victims and 1 in 13 male murder victims are killed by intimate partners.

72% of all murder-suicides involve an intimate partner.

94% of the victims of these murder-suicides are female.

Most intimate partner homicides are committed with firearms.

Abusers' access to firearms increases the risk of intimate partner femicide at least five-fold. When firearms have been used in the most severe abuse incident, the risk increases 41-fold.

While the overall rate of intimate partner has decreased, intimate partner femicide has increased in recent years, driven by an increase in intimate partner femicide committed with a firearm.

Children and Domestic Violence

The National Survey of Children's Exposure to Violence found that 1 in 15 children in the United States had been exposed to physical intimate partner violence in the previous year and 5.7% were exposed to psychological intimate partner violence in the previous year.

Approximately one in five children witness intimate partner violence in their lifetimes.

Witnessing intimate partner violence is associated with other forms of violence. Almost 60% of children who witnessed domestic violence also experienced child maltreatment in their lifetimes.

More than 70% of victims of child sex abuse by a known adult also witnessed intimate partner violence.

Half of children who experience child maltreatment also witness intimate partner violence.

Child maltreatment that co-occurs with intimate partner violence tends to be more severe than child maltreatment without co-occurring intimate partner violence.

A one-day snapshot of service usage in 80% of shelters in 2021 found that the second-most common service provided by domestic violence programs was children's support or advocacy, second only to emergency shelters. On that day, 20,233 children lived in emergency shelters, transitional housing, or a hotel/motel, and another 5,461 received non-residential services.

Children's immediate reaction to experiencing domestic violence include generalized anxiety, sleeplessness, aggression, difficulty concentrating, nightmares, bed-wetting, and separation anxiety.

Abusers may abuse children as part of the abuse of the intimate partner. Abusive partners use children to control victims. Abusive partners often threaten to gain sole custody, kill, kidnap or otherwise harm children if victims leave.

Children who witness intimate partner violence growing up are three times as likely as their peers to engage in violent behavior and to be engaged in a variety of violent and non-violent crime.

Children raised in abusive homes learn that violence is an appropriate way to solve conflict. These children are more likely than their peers to be in abusive intimate partner relationships in the future, either as victims or perpetrators.

Children who witness incidents of domestic violence (a form of childhood trauma) are at greater risk of serious adult health problems including obesity, cancer, heart disease, depression, substance abuse, tobacco use and unintended pregnancies than peers who did not witness domestic violence.

Economic Impact

Victims of intimate partner violence lose a total of 8.0 million days of paid work each year, the equivalent of 32,000 full-time jobs.

The cost of intimate partner violence is estimated to cost the US economy between $5.8 billion and $12.6 billion annually, up to 0.125% of the national gross domestic product.

Between 21-60% of victims of intimate partner violence lose their jobs due to reasons stemming from the abuse.

Between 2003 and 2008, 142 women were murdered in their workplace by former or current intimate partners. This amounts to 22% of workplace homicides among women.

Physical and Mental Impact

Women abused by their intimate partners are more vulnerable to contracting HIV or other STI's due to forced intercourse or prolonged exposure to stress.

Studies suggest that there is a relationship between intimate partner violence and depression and suicidal behavior.

Physical, mental, and sexual and reproductive health effects have been linked with intimate partner violence including adolescent pregnancy, unintended pregnancy in general, miscarriage, stillbirth, intrauterine hemorrhage, nutritional deficiency, abdominal pain and other gastrointestinal problems, neurological disorders, chronic pain, disability, anxiety and post-traumatic stress disorder (PTSD), as well as noncommunicable diseases such as hypertension, cancer and cardiovascular diseases. Victims of domestic violence are also at higher risk for developing addictions to alcohol, tobacco, or drugs.

Misfits

CLOTHING BOUTIQUE

misfitsclothingboutique.com

forWord Books

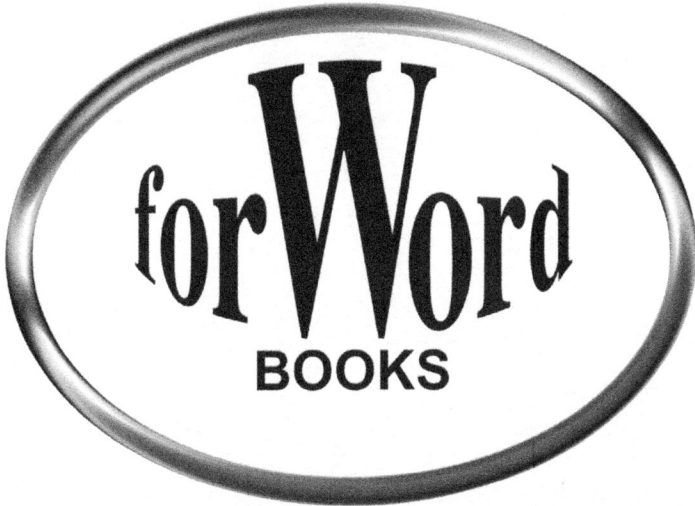

John 1:1 In the beginning was the Word...

A CHRISTIAN BOOK PUBLISHING COMPANY

CONTACT US VIA EMAIL AT
FORWORDBOOKS@GMAIL.COM

Made in the USA
Las Vegas, NV
19 May 2024